1001
Most Useful
FRENCH
Words
NEW EDITION

Heather McCoy, Ph.D.

DOVER PUBLICATIONS, INC.
Mineola, New York

Copyright

Bibliographical Note

1001 Most Useful French Words NEW EDITION, first published by Dover Publications, Inc., in 2012, is a new selection of material from *2,001 Useful French Words,* published in 2010 by Dover Publications, Inc.

Library of Congress Cataloging-in-Publication Data

McCoy, Heather.
    1001 most useful French words / Heather McCoy. — New ed.
        p. cm.
    "1001 Most Useful French Words New Edition, first published by Dover Publications, Inc., in 2012, is a new selection of material from 2,001 Useful French Words, published in 2010 by Dover Publications, Inc."—T.p. verso.
    Text in English and French.
    ISBN-13: 978-0-486-49898-0
    ISBN-10: 0-486-49898-0
    1. French language—Vocabulary. 2. French language—Usage. 3. French language—Grammar. I. McCoy, Heather. 2,001 most useful French words. II. Title. III. Title: One thousand and one most useful French words.

PC2445.M325 2012
448.2'421—dc23

                                                                        2012030153

Manufactured in the United States by Courier Corporation
49898001
www.doverpublications.com

Contents

Acknowledgments

I would like to thank those who have assisted me with this project, directly and indirectly. I gratefully acknowledge Rochelle Kronzek and Janet Kopito, editors at Dover Publications, for the opportunity to create a book that allowed me to immerse myself in the glory of words; Sandrine Siméon, for her careful proofreading and helpful suggestions; Bénédicte Monicat, for being a stellar colleague; the students at Penn State University, who continue to teach me so much; and my husband, Gary J. Weisel, whose sense of dedication to hard work will always be a source of inspiration to me.

Introduction

This book is intended for anyone who wishes to enrich his or her French vocabulary. Readers will find a review of well-known terms, as well as many new and useful words. The structure of the book permits it to be used in a variety of ways, either alphabetically for a systematic review, or randomly, to dip in for a casual perusal. This flexibility will contribute to the book's usefulness.

The first section of the book contains an alphabetical listing of all 1001 words. Each word is listed in French, with the English translation immediately following. The gender of nouns is indicated as masculine (m.) or feminine (f.); plural nouns are indicated as well (pl.). Adjectives are provided in the masculine form with the feminine form indicated in parentheses. In addition, each word is presented in a French sentence for context, followed by the English translation.

The second part of the book contains a Categories section. Here you will find simple vocabulary reference lists of common words that will be useful to you when you want to describe yourself, talk about your family, communicate while traveling, and many other purposes. These are terms that you have likely learned before—most of them are straightforward enough that contextual information isn't provided.

A word about context: One of the most important tools we have for discerning meaning in language is context. This is true for our native language, as well as for languages we learn as non-native speakers. You might not know what the word "punctilious" means in English, but when you see the sentence "I can think of no better way to describe Margaret than "punctilious"—she shows the highest regard for correct behavior, and proper etiquette is always her primary concern," the meaning of "punctilious" will be clear. You can figure out from the context that "punctilious" likely means *socially correct* and *mindful of good manners and conventions*. A word can also mean very different things depending on the words around it. The sentences "This sweater is green" and "My cousin is interested in green technologies" use the word "green" in different ways, and it is the rest of the sentence that makes the intended meaning evident. In this book we are limited to contextual clues at the sentence level, but in the world beyond this book, contextual clues reach far beyond the sentence. Elements such as the age of the speaker(s), the person who is being addressed (and by whom), the place where these words are being uttered, and even whether humor is intended, all offer potential contextual clues for meaning. Keep this in mind when you hear the words in this book being used in new or unexpected ways.

We believe that *1001 Most Useful French Words NEW EDITION* will provide an eminently useful tool, however you choose to use it. Our goal is for this handy book to be an indispensable tool in your further explorations in the French language. Immerse yourself in the pleasure of the words as you read it. *Bonne lecture!*

French Pronunciation Guide

Here are some general principles of pronunciation:

Nasalization

In French, a vowel is nasalized when it is followed by a single *m* or *n* in the same syllable. The transcription of these nasalized vowels appears as:

-an, -am, -em, -en -> ahn, ehn
-in, -im -> ihn, ihm
-on, -om -> ohn, ohm
-um, -un -> uhn

To produce a nasalized vowel, quickly pass the air through both the nose and the mouth at the same time. The *m* or *n* isn't pronounced after the nasal vowel, as follows:

français -> frahn-say ; *temps* -> tahn
pain -> pihn ; *printemps* ->prihn-tehn
bon -> bohn
quelqu'un -> kell-kuhn

Silent Final Consonants

In French, most consonants at the end of a word are silent, although there are exceptions to this rule: *c*, *f*, and *l*. The consonant *r* also is pronounced, but is silent when occurring in the endings *-er* and *-ier*.

The French r

The French *r* can be one of the most challenging sounds for English speakers to pronounce. Pronunciation of the *r* will depend upon the region of the French-speaking world that you are visiting. In some areas, the French *r* can resemble the Italian or Spanish *r*—produced by rolling it on the tip of the tongue. The Parisian *r* is a more gutteral sound: it's helpful to imagine the sound being produced in the back of the throat, the same place that produces the *h* in "ahoy." The *r* is voiced, meaning that there is a slight vibration of the vocal chords.

The Plural s

As mentioned above, consonants at the end of words normally are not pronounced. Make special note of this when pronouncing the *s* that denotes the plural:

Le chat -> luh shah
Les chats -> lay shah

Notice how the pronunciation of the noun *chat* does not change between the singular and the plural. This is quite different from English, and is important for English speakers to remember.

Liaison

A final consonant that is normally silent is pronounced when it comes before a vowel or *h*. This phenomenon is called *liaison*. Note the following change:

A final *s* before a consonant: *des livres* -> day leev-ruh
A final *s* before a vowel: *des animaux* -> daze ehn-ee-moh
The rules for liaison can be somewhat complex, so simply pay attention to the phonetic transcriptions in order to get a feel for when its usage is appropriate.

Stress

The last syllable of a French word is usually stressed:

Beaucoup -> boh-<u>koo</u>

However, when the last syllable is an unstressed *e* (*uh* in the transcription used here), the next-to-the-last syllable receives the stress:

Formidable -> for-mee-<u>dah</u>-bluh

You will also notice that in addition to the stress at the end of a word, there also is stress at the end of a phrase:

Je suis américain et travaille au musée d'art contemporain. -> zhuh swee <u>za</u>-mary-<u>kihn</u> ay tra-vy oh moo-<u>zay</u> <u>dar</u> cohn-<u>tehn</u>-por-<u>ihn</u>.

Scheme of Pronunciation

Letters	Transcription	Example	Notes
a	a	as in *ask*, but cut short	
	ah	as in *father*	
ai	ay	as in *play*	
	y	as in *why*	
au	oh	as in *bow*	See note on *o* below.
b	b	as in *bear*	
c	k	as in *car*	Pronounced *k* before *a*, *o*, or *u*
	s	as in *sun*	Pronounced *s* before *e* and *i*
ç	s	as in *sun*	
d	d	as in *danger*	Formed by touching tongue tip to teeth
e, è	eh	as in *met*	
é	ay	as in *play*	

e, eu, œu	uh	as in *bubble*	
f	f	as in *fan*	
g	g	as in *give*	Before *a*, *o*, and *u*
g	zh	as in *garage*	Before *e* and *i*
gn	ny	as in *canyon*	
h	silent		
i	ee	as in *feet*	
j	zh	as in *garage*	
k	k	as in *kernel*	
l	l	as in *lap*	
m	m	as in *me*	
n	n	as in *note*	
o	oh	as in *toe*	
oi	wa	as in *want*	
ou	oo	as in *boom*	
p	p	as in *pat*	
ph	f	as in *fan*	
q	k	as in *kernel*	
r	r	as in *red*	See section above.
s	ss	as in *lass*	At the beginning of the word or when doubled
	z	as in *zap*	When between two vowels
	silent		At the end of a word, unless followed by a vowel. See section above.
t	t	as in *tip*	
th	t	as in *tip*	

u	oo	no English equivalent	Formed by saying "ee," moving lips into rounded position without moving tongue.
v	v	as in *vote*	
w	v, w	as in *vote, win*	
x	ks	as in *licks*	
y	ee	as in *greet*	
z	z	as in *zoo*	

Alphabetical Section

A

à   *in, at, to*
Je dois aller à la mairie pour récupérer des documents.
I need to go to the town hall to pick up some documents.

absent(e)   *absent*
Il est souvent absent de notre classe.
He's frequently absent from our class.

absolument   *absolutely*
Il faut absolument que tu m'appelles demain.
You absolutely must call me tomorrow.

accepter   *to accept*
Le gouvernement accepte la responsabilité des problèmes du pays.
The government accepts responsibility for the country's problems.

accès m.   *access*
L'accès aux quais est interdit.
Access to the platforms is forbidden.

accompagner   *to accompany, go with*
Je peux vous accompagner?
May I accompany you?

accord m.   *accord, agreement*
Est-ce qu'il a donné son accord pour le projet?
Did he give his agreement for the project?

achat m.   *purchase*
Je sais que ce sac est un achat impulsif mais, je l'adore!
I know this handbag was an impulse purchase, but I love it!

acheter   *to buy*
Elle veut acheter cette voiture, mais elle n'a pas assez d'argent.
She wants to buy this car but doesn't have enough money.

action f.   *action.*
Mon cousin aime bien les films d'action.
My cousin loves action films.

actuel(le)   *present, current*
Quel est l'état actuel de la situation politique dans votre pays?
What is the current state of the political situation in your country?

actuellement   *currently, at the time being*
On a peu de travail actuellement.
We have little work at the time being.

adapter   *to adapt*
Le cinéaste désire adapter cette pièce au cinéma.
The filmmaker wants to adapt this play for film.

addition f.   *bill, check*
L'addition, s'il vous plaît!
The check, please!

adopter   *to adopt*
L'Assemblé nationale a décidé d'adopter cette nouvelle loi.
The National Assembly decided to adopt this new law.

adorer   *to adore, love*
Il adore les langues; il veut devenir prof de langues.
He loves languages; he wants to be a language teacher.

adresse f.   *address*
Quelle est votre adresse?
What's your address?

aéroport m.   *airport*
Ma navette part pour l'aéroport dans trois quarts d'heure.
My shuttle leaves for the airport in forty-five minutes.

affaire f.   *affair, matter*
Sois prudent, c'est une affaire louche.
Be careful, it's a shady deal.

affaires m. pl.   *business, business dealings*
Mon oncle est expert en affaires internationales.
My uncle is an expert in international business.

affectueux(-euse)   *affectionate*
Elle est toujours très affectueuse avec ses enfants.
She's always very affectionate with her children.

afin de / afin que *in order to / so that*
Marc a pris un taxi afin d'arriver à l'heure à son rendez-vous.
Marc took a taxi in order to arrive at his appointment on time.

âge m. *age*
Elle a quel âge?
How old is she?

agence de voyages f. *travel agency*
Je dois passer par l'agence de voyages afin d'acheter mon billet
de train.
I need to stop by the travel agency to buy my train ticket.

agent *(de police)* m. *police officer.*
Il y a un agent de police à l'appareil qui veut te parler!
There's a police office on the phone who wants to talk to you!

agréable *agreeable, pleasant*
On a passé un après-midi agréable au jardin botanique.
We spent a pleasant afternoon at the botanical garden.

agriculteur m. *farmer*
Mon oncle est agriculteur dans le Morvan.
My uncle is a farmer in the Morvan region.

aider *to help*
Je peux vous aider?
May I help you?

ailleurs; d'ailleurs *elsewhere; besides, moreover*
On n'a pas réussi à l'examen, et d'ailleurs je dois admettre qu'on
n'a même pas étudié!
*We didn't pass the test, and moreover, I must admit that we didn't even
study!*

aimable *nice, pleasant*
Notre nouveau collègue est assez aimable, en fait.
Our new colleague is, in fact, pretty nice.

aimer *to love;* **aimer bien** *to like*
J'aime bien le jazz. Et toi?
I like jazz. And you?

air m. *air*
On va à l'exterieur pour prendre de l'air.
We're going outside to get some fresh air.

ajouter   *to add*
Je n'ai rien à ajouter à cette discussion.
I don't have anything to add to this discussion.

aller   *to go*
Tu n'as pas envie d'y aller?
You don't feel like going there?

allumer   *to light, to turn on, to ignite*
Peux-tu allumer le gaz?
Can you turn on the gas?

alors   *so, then, therefore*
Alors, ça s'est bien passé?
So, did it go well?

ami(e) m. (f.)   *friend*
Ça fait longtemps qu'on n'a pas vu notre ami Pierre.
We haven't seen our friend Peter for a long time.

amical(e)   *friendly*
On a eu une conversation assez amicale hier.
We had a friendly enough conversation yesterday.

amitié f.   *friendship*
L'amitié est très importante pour les adolescents.
Friendship is very important to adolescents.

amour m.   *love*
La conception de l'amour dans cette culture est très différente de
    la nôtre.
The concept of love in this culture is very different from ours.

amoureux(-euse)   *in love*
Il est amoureux d'elle.
He's in love with her.

ampleur f.   *size, scope*
Un problème de cette ampleur doit être pris en considération avant
    de procéder.
A problem of this scope should be taken into consideration before proceeding.

amuser, s'   *to have a good time, to enjoy oneself*
On s'est vraiment amusé chez nos voisins hier soir.
We had a really good time at our neighbors' house last night.

an m.   *year*
On a vu notre grand-père il y a trois ans à Angers.
We saw our grandfather three years ago in Angers.

anglais m.   *English*
Tu parles bien l'anglais.
You speak English well.

anglais(e)   *English*
Je viens de voir un film anglais qui m'a beaucoup impressionné.
I've just seen an English film that really impressed me.

Angleterre f.   *England*
J'ai très envie de visiter l'Angleterre l'été prochain.
I'm really eager to visit England next summer.

animé(e)   *lively, animated*
On peut toujours compter sur Monique pour avoir un repas
    animé chez elle.
We can always count on Monique to have a lively meal at her place.

anniversaire m.   *birthday*
Elle m'a donné un pull pour mon anniversaire.
She gave me a sweater for my birthday.

annonce f.   *notice, advertisement*
Si vous voulez changer votre nom, il faut l'indiquer dans une
    annonce dans le journal.
*If you want to change your name, you have to put it in a notice in the
    newspaper.*

appareil m.   *appliance, camera*
Elle veut prendre des photos avec son nouvel appareil photo.
She wants to take pictures with her new camera.

appartement, appart (colloq.) m.   *apartment*
Tu devrais voir le nouvel appart de Jean-Marie, c'est incroyable!
You should see Jean-Marie's new apartment, it's incredible!

appartenir   *to belong*
Ce sac n'appartient à personne.
This bag doesn't belong to anyone.

appeler   *to call*
Il va nous appeler avec les directions.
He's going to call us with the directions.

appeler, s'   *to be named*
Je m'appelle François, et vous?
My name is Frank. And yours?

apporter   *to bring*
Tu devrais apporter ton écran-solaire sur la plage.
You should bring your sunblock to the beach.

apprendre   *to learn*
On apprend à faire du snowboard.
We're learning to snowboard.

apprêter   *to prepare, to dispose someone to something*
Elle apprête un repas pour nous.
She is preparing a meal for us.

après   *after*
Si on allait boire un coup après le film?
How about getting a drink after the movie?

après-midi m.   *afternoon*
Cet après-midi j'espère pouvoir lire le journal.
This afternoon I hope to be able to read the newspaper.

arbre m.   *tree*
Dans notre jardin il y a un arbre qui fleurit.
There's a flowering tree in our garden.

argent m.   *money*
Tu peux me prêter de l'argent?
Can you lend me some money?

arriere, en   *behind*
Il a fait un pas en arrière.
He took a step back.

arrière-goût m.   *aftertaste*
Ce fromage bleu a un arrière-goût assez désagréable.
This blue cheese has a somewhat disagreeable aftertaste.

arrivée f.   *arrival*
On attend avec impatience l'arrivée de la délégation chinoise.
We're impatiently awaiting the arrival of the Chinese delegation.

arriver   *to arrive*
Le train arrive à 10h45.
The train is arriving at 10:45 a.m.

art m.   *art*
Je m'intéresse surtout à l'art abstrait.
I'm mainly interested in abstract art.

article m.   *article*
Je viens de lire un article au sujet de la situation politique de
   notre pays.
I just read an article about the political situation of our country.

asseoir, s'   *to sit down*
Vous pouvez vous asseoir.
You may sit down.

assez de   *enough (of)*
Je n'ai pas assez de farine pour cette recette.
I don't have enough flour for this recipe.

assumer   *to assume, to take on*
Désormais il va assumer toutes les responsabilités.
From now on he's going to take on all responsibilities.

assurer   *to assure, to insure*
Je peux vous assurer que notre entreprise fera face à cette crise.
I can assure you that our company will handle this crisis.

atout m.   *asset, advantage, trump card*
Ce diplôme sera un atout professionnel quand vous chercherez
   du travail.
This degree will be a professional asset when you look for work.

attention f.   *attention*
Le prof attire l'attention de la classe sur les devoirs pour
   mercredi.
*The professor draws the class's attention to the assignments due
   Wednesday.*

attention f. (exclamation)   *attention, care*
Attention!
Watch out!

attirer   *to attract*
Je pense que ce nouveau café va attirer beaucoup d'attention.
I think that this new café will attract a lot of attention.

aucun(e)   *none*
Aucun étudiant n'est prêt pour l'examen.
No student is ready for the test.

aujourd'hui   *today*
Elles partent aujourd'hui pour deux semaines en Tunisie.
They're leaving today for two weeks in Tunisia.

aussi   *also, too*
On va visiter Rennes, Rouen et Quimper aussi, si on a le temps.
We're going to visit Rennes, Rouen, and Quimper, too, if we have the time.

autant de   *so much / so many*
Je n'ai jamais eu autant de cadeaux pour mon anniversaire!
I have never had so many gifts for my birthday!

autocar m.   *intercity bus, coach*
Au lieu de prendre le train, je préfère voyager en autocar.
Instead of taking the train, I prefer to take the intercity bus.

autorité f.   *authority*
Vous n'avez pas l'autorité de prendre cette décision.
You don't have the authority to make this decision.

autoroute f.   *highway*
Les camionneurs préfèrent rouler sur les autoroutes la nuit quand il y a peu de circulation.
Truck drivers prefer to drive on highways at night when there is not much traffic.

autour de   *around, about*
Le vendredi soir ma famille et moi faisons une promenade autour de la Place St. Marc.
On Friday nights my family and I take a walk around St. Marc's Square.

autre   *other, another*
Je peux voir une autre couleur, s'il vous plaît?
May I see another color, please?

autres, les   *the rest, the others*
Vous pouvez venir chez moi mais les autres doivent rester ici.
You can come to my place but the others must stay here.

avant de   *before*
Tu devrais lire le livre avant de le critiquer!
You should read the book before criticizing it!

avec   *with*
Est-ce qu'ils veulent travailler avec nous?
Do they want to work with us?

avenue f.   *avenue*
L'avenue des Champs-Elysées est bien connue dans le monde entier.
The Avenue of the Champs-Elysées is well known the world over.

avertissement m.   *warning, notification*
Il vient de nous donner l'avertissement que notre immeuble sera bientôt vendu.
He just gave us notification that our building soon will be sold.

avion m.   *airplane*
L'agent de voyage nous recommande de voyager par avion.
The travel agent recommends that we travel by airplane.

avoir   *to have*
Ce soir je vais avoir quelques amies chez moi pour une petite fête.
Tonight I'm going to have a few friends over for a small party.

avouer   *to admit*
Je dois avouer que mes enfants n'ont jamais mangé de chocolat!
I must admit that my kids have never eaten chocolate!

B

bac m.   *baccalaureate degree that permits one to enter the university system in France.*
Elle a échoué au bac donc elle doit retenter l'examen l'année prochaine.
She failed the baccalaureate exam, so she has to retry the exam next year.

bâcler   *to botch*
L'artiste n'a pas fait attention et il a bâclé son ouvrage.
The artist didn't pay attention and botched his work.

bagage m.   *bag, baggage*
On peut laisser nos bagages à la consigne, n'est-ce pas?
We can leave our bags at the baggage checkroom, right?

bagatelle f.   *trifle, small matter*
Il parlait de son problème comme si ce n'était qu'une bagatelle.
He was talking about his problem as if it was only a small matter.

bague f.   *ring*
Hier j'ai retrouvé la bague que j'avais perdue il y a un an!
Yesterday I found the ring that I had lost a year ago!

baiser, donner un m.   *to give a kiss*
Chaque matin ma mère me donne un baiser avant d'aller au
travail.
Each morning my mom gives me a kiss before leaving for work.

baisser   *to lower*
Baisse tes phares quand tu conduis ici, sinon tu vas aveugler les
autres conducteurs.
*Lower your headlights when you drive here; if you don't, you'll blind
the other drivers.*

bal m.   *a ball, dance*
Tu as besoin de trouver un bon déguisement pour le bal masqué.
You need to find a good costume for the costume ball.

balader, se   *to go for a stroll*
J'aime bien me balader quand je me sens stressé.
I like to go for a stroll when I am feeling stressed.

banlieue f.   *suburb*
Le jeune couple rêve de quitter la banlieue.
The young couple dreams about getting out of the suburbs.

banque f.   *bank*
Sandrine vient d'ouvrir un compte d'épargne à la banque.
Sandrine just opened a savings account at the bank.

bas(se)   *low*
Le plafond dans ce salon est un peu trop bas à mon avis.
The ceiling in this living room is a bit too low, in my opinion.

bas (en)   *downstairs, below*
Attendez-nous en bas, s'il vous plaît.
Please wait for us downtairs.

bateau m.   *boat*
L'année dernière on a pris le bateau Sète-Maroc. Quel voyage
inoubliable!
*Last year we took the boat from Sète to Morocco. What an unforgettable
trip!*

bavarder   *to chatter, to gossip*
Les deux élèves n'arrêtaient pas de bavarder pendant le cours.
The two pupils didn't stop chattering during class.

beau(belle) (**bel** in front of a vowel and *h*)   *beautiful*
Quel beau chat!
What a beautiful cat!

Quelle belle idée!
What a beautiful idea!
Quel bel hôtel!
What a beautiful hotel!

beaucoup   *a lot*
Il faut avoir beaucoup de patience avec les enfants.
It's necessary to have a lot of patience with children.

besoin de, avoir   *to need*
Ils ont besoin d'aller à la banque avant qu'elle ne ferme.
They need to go to the bank before it closes.

bête   *stupid, dumb*
Parfois je te trouve vraiment bête, tu sais.
You know, sometimes I think you're really stupid.

beurre m.   *butter*
Achetons du beurre à la crémerie.
Let's buy some butter at the dairy store.

bibliothèque f.   *library*
Si tu passais plus de temps à la bibliothèque, tu aurais plus de
   succès dans tes cours, tu sais.
*If you spent more time at the library, you would have more success in
   your courses, you know.*

bien   *well*
Elle écrit bien le grec mais elle a du mal à le parler.
She writes Greek well but has difficulty speaking it.

bien que   *although*
Bien que je me sois amélioré, je n'ai pas progressé autant que je
   l'aurais espéré.
*Although I've improved, I haven't progressed as much as I would've
   liked.*

bientôt   *soon*
Ils auront bientôt suffisament d'argent pour acheter une
   maisonnette à la campagne.
They'll soon have enough money to buy a small cottage in the country.

bienvenu(e)   *welcome*
Madame Siméon, soyez la bienvenue!
Welcome, Madame Siméon!

bijou(x) m. (pl.)   *jewel, gem*
   Ce livre est un vrai bijou.
   This book really is a gem.
   Je viens de retrouver les bijoux de mon arrière-grand-mère, ils
      sont incroyables!
   I just found my great grandmother's jewels. They're incredible!

billet m.   *ticket*
   S'il te faut un billet pas cher, je te conseille de chercher sur
      Internet.
   If you need a cheap ticket, I advise you to look on the Internet.

bistrot, bistro m.   *café, pub, small restaurant*
   Je veux te présenter à mes amis qui travaillent dans le bistrot du
      coin.
   *I want to introduce you to my friends who work in the small restaurant
   on the corner.*

blague f.   *joke*
   Il raconte toujours des blagues ridicules.
   He always tells ridiculous jokes.

blanc(-he)   *white*
   La mariée portait une robe blanche.
   The bride wore a white dress.

blanchir   *to whiten, to bleach*
   On va essayer de blanchir cette chemise jaunie.
   We're going to try to whiten this yellowed blouse.

blesser   *to hurt, to injure, to wound*
   Le soldat a été blessé pendant la guerre.
   The soldier was wounded during the war.

bleu(e)   *blue*
   Ne mets pas un cardigan bleu avec cette robe rouge, ça cloche!
   Don't wear a blue cardigan with this red dress. It clashes!

boire   *to drink*
   Le médecin m'a dit de boire moins de gin et plus d'eau.
   The doctor told me to drink less gin and more water.

bois m.   *wood, the woods*
   Ma mère vient de fabriquer une cabane à oiseaux tout en bois.
   My mom just made a birdhouse entirely out of wood.
   L'après-midi on aime bien se promener dans les bois.
   We like to take walks in the woods every afternoon.

boisson f.   *drink, beverage*
Quel est ta boisson préférée?
What's your favorite drink?

boîte f.   *box, can*
Tu peux acheter une boîte de sardines à l'épicerie?
Can you buy a can of sardines at the corner store?

bon(-ne)   *good*
Elle a un très bon ordinateur.
She has a very good computer.
J'espère que tu passeras une bonne journée à la foire.
I hope you have a good day at the fair.

bon marché   *cheap, low-cost, inexpensive*
Il a eu ses chaussures à bon marché.
He got his shoes for an inexpensive price.

bordélique   *(colloquial) messy, chaotic*
Mon appart est tellement bordélique que je veux pas retourner
    chez moi!
My apartment is so messy that I can't stand to go home!

bordure f.   *border, edge*
On a garé notre voiture en bordure de la fôret.
We parked our car at the edge of the forest.

bouche f.   *mouth*
Cette tarte me fait venir l'eau à la bouche!
This pie makes my mouth water!

bouchée f.   *mouthful*
J'ai pris une bouchée de ta tarte, elle est délicieuse!
I took a mouthful of your pie, it's delicious!

bouffe f.   *(colloquial) food*
J'aime bien la bouffe ici.
I really like the food here.

bouquin m.   *book (familiar)*
On a acheté un vieux bouquin au marché aux puces.
We bought an old book at the flea market.

bourse f.   *the stock exchange*
Ces actions ne sont pas cotées à la Bourse de New York.
These stocks aren't listed on the New York Stock Exchange.

bouteille f.   *bottle*
Ils ont acheté trois bouteilles de vin blanc pour la fête.
They bought three bottles of white wine for the party.

bras m.   *arm*
Depuis le match de rugby d'hier, Jean-Claude a vraiment mal au bras.
Jean-Claude's arm really hurts since yesterday's rugby match.

bref   *in short*
Bref, on a eu toutes sortes de problèmes.
In short, we had all sorts of problems.

bricolage m.   *DIY, do-it-yourself hobbies*
Pour completer ce projet on a dû faire du bricolage.
To complete this project we had to do a bit of DIY.

brièvement   *briefly, brief*
Explique-moi brièvement ton problème!
Give me a brief explanation of your problem.

brouiller   *to blur, to confuse*
Toutes ces informations brouillaient mes idées.
All of this information confused me.

bruit m.   *noise*
On a soudainement eu peur parce qu'on a entendu un bruit fort à l'extérieur.
We suddenly became scared because we heard a loud noise outside.

brûler   *to burn*
Sandra va dîner au restaurant parce que Mathias a brûlé leur repas.
Sandra is going to have dinner at the restaurant because Mathias burnt their meal.

brûlure f.   *burn*
J'ai une brûlure sur le cou et ça fait mal!
I have a burn on my neck and it hurts!

brun(e)   *brown*
Mon père est brun et sa mère était brune aussi.
My dad has brown hair, and his mother was a brunette as well.

brusque   *abrupt, sudden*
Je n'apprécie pas votre ton brusque, Mademoiselle.
I don't appreciate your abrupt tone, Miss.

bruyant(e)   *noisy, loud*
Il est très bruyant comme bébé, il ne se tait jamais.
He's a very noisy baby—he's never quiet.

bureau m.   *office*
Elle travaille tard et ne quitte jamais le bureau avant onze heures du soir.
She works late and never leaves the office before eleven o'clock at night.

but m.   *goal, purpose*
Je ne vois pas très bien le but de cette question, que veux-tu savoir exactement?
I don't really understand the point of this question—what do you want to know exactly?

C

ça   *that*
Ça, c'est mon livre préféré.
That's my favorite book.

cacahuète f.   *peanut*
Notre fils est allergique aux cacahuètes.
Our son is allergic to peanuts.

cacher   *to conceal*
Elle a du mal à cacher ses sentiments.
She has a hard time hiding her feelings.

cadeau m.   *present*
Ils vont offrir un cadeau d'anniversaire à leur collègue qui fête ses 70 ans.
They're going to give a birthday present to their colleague, who is celebrating her seventieth birthday.

cadre m.   *frame, setting, framework; executive*
Mettons cette photo dans un cadre.
Let's put this picture in a frame.
Les cadres de cette entreprise sont bien payés.
The executives of this firm are well paid.

café m.   *coffee*
Si on prenait un café?
How about getting some coffee?

café m.   *café*
Il y a café charmant que tous les étudiants fréquentent. Tu veux y aller?
There's a charming café that all the students go to. Do you want to go there?

cafétéria f.   *cafeteria*
On a fini par déjeuner à la cafeteria parce qu'on n'avait pas le temps d'aller au restaurant.
We ended up eating at the cafeteria because we didn't have the time to go to a restaurant.

cahier m.   *workbook, notebook*
La classe doit faire trois exercises de grammaire dans le cahier pour demain.
The class has to do three grammar exercises in the workbook for tomorrow.

caisse f.   *cash register, checkout*
Avant de quitter le magasin, je dois régler à la caisse.
Before leaving the store, I have to pay at the cash register.

caissier(-ière) m. (f.)   *cashier, checkout employee*
Le weekend elle travaille comme caissière.
She works weekends as a cashier.

calculatrice f.   *calculator*
Je suis nulle en maths donc je me sers toujours d'une calculatrice.
I'm terrible at math so I always use a calculator.

calme   *calm*
C'est bizarre que la mer soit si calme après tant d'orages.
It's odd that the sea is co calm after so many storms.

calmer, se   *to calm oneself, to calm down*
Calmez-vous Madame, vous n'avez pas à vous inquiéter!
Calm down, ma'am, you don't need to get so worried!

caméra f.   *video or movie camera*
Le couple a acheté une caméra pour filmer sa lune de miel.
The couple bought a video camera to film their honeymoon.

campagne f.   *the countryside*
Moi je préfère la montagne à la campagne.
Personally, I prefer the mountains to the countryside.

canapé m.   *couch, sofa*
On a acheté ce canapé-là à un très bon prix.
We bought this couch for a really good price.

canicule f.   *heat wave*
On souffre de la canicule depuis deux semaines.
We have been suffering from a heat wave for two weeks.

capitale f.   *capital (city)*
Quelle est la capitale de la France?
What is the capital of France?

carnet m.   *book of tickets, notebook*
Comme vous êtes à Paris pour seulement une journée, vous
    devriez acheter un carnet de dix tickets.
*Since you're only in Paris for one day, you should buy a book of ten
    tickets.*

carrefour m.   *crossroads, intersection, forum*
La France est le carrefour de l'Europe.
France is the crossroads of Europe.
On organise un carrefour d'idées lors de notre congrès.
We are organizing a forum to be held at the time of our convention.

carrière f.   *career*
Mon neveu ne sait pas du tout ce qu'il veut faire comme carrière.
My nephew doesn't know at all what he wants to do for a career.

carte f.   *card, map, menu*
J'ai envoyé une carte de vœux à mon ancien prof.
I sent a greeting card to my former teacher.
Donne-moi la carte pour que je te montre notre ville.
Give me the map so I can point out our town.
Il n'y a rien sur la carte qui m'intéresse.
There is nothing on the menu that interests me.

casque m.   *helmet*
Elle ne permet pas à ses enfants de faire du vélo sans casque.
She doesn't let her kids ride their bikes without a helmet.

casse-croûte m.   *snack*
Veux-tu du jus d'orange avec ton casse-croûte?
Do you want some orange juice with your snack?

casser   *to break*
Il s'est cassé le bras en skiant.
He broke his arm while skiing.

catholique   *Catholic*
L'Italie est un pays très catholique.
Italy is a very Catholic country.

causer   *to cause*
Qu'est-ce qui a causé tous ces problèmes?
What has caused all these problems?

causer   *to chat*
Causons de nos inquiétudes pour que l'on se sente mieux.
Let's talk about our troubles so we feel better.

ce, cette, ces (**cet** *in front of a vowel*)   *this, these*
Ce chat / cette maison/ cet homme / est adorable comme tout.
This cat/house/man is adorable as anything.
Ces tasses à café doivent être rangées dans le placard.
These coffee cups need to be put away in the cupboard.

ceinture f.   *belt*
Mets ta a ceinture de sécurité!
Put on your seat belt!

célèbre   *famous, well-known*
Phèdre est la pièce la plus célèbre de Racine.
Phèdre is Racine's most famous play.

célibataire   *single*
Je ne suis pas marié; je préfère rester célibataire.
I'm not married; I prefer to stay single.

celle(s)   *the one, those*
Celle qui arrivera en premier gagnera une récompense.
The one who arrives (there) first will win a prize.

celui(ceux)   *the one, those*
Tu préfères celui en vert ou celui en orange?
Do you prefer the green one or the orange one?
Ceux qui n'auront pas fini leurs devoirs n'auront pas le droit de
sortir ce soir.
*Those who haven't finished their assignments won't have the right to go
out tonight.*

centre-ville m.   *downtown*
Et si on faisait du lèche-vitrine au centre-ville?
How about some window-shopping downtown?

certain(e)   *certain, sure, definite*
Cet homme-là est méchant, c'est certain, mais parfois il est aussi très généreux.
That man is mean, that's for sure, but sometimes he's also quite generous.

certainement   *certainly, for certain*
On arrivera certainement avant toi.
We'll certainly arrive before you.

cesser   *to stop*
Elle est tellement bavarde, elle ne cesse de parler.
She's so talkative, she never stops speaking.

chacun(e)   *each one*
Il faut donner le même examen à chacun.
You have to give the same exam to each one.

chaise f.   *chair*
Je trouve que cette chaise rouge na va pas du tout dans ce salon bleu.
I think that this red chair doesn't go at all with this blue living room.

chaleur f.   *heat*
Quelle chaleur! Allons à la piscine.
What heat! Let's go to the pool.

chambre f.   *bedroom*
Quand Sandra était petite, elle partageait sa chambre avec ses deux petites sœurs.
When Sandra was little, she shared her room with her two younger sisters.

champ m.   *field*
L'agriculteur est dans son champ en train de planifier les prochaines récoltes.
The farmer is in his field planning his next crops.

chance f.   *luck*
Décidemment tu n'as pas de chance!
Clearly you have bad luck!

changer   *to changer*
Est-il jamais possible de vraiment changer quelqu'un?
Is it ever really possible to change someone?

chanson f.　　*song*
Les chansons de Serge Gainsbourg sont un peu coquines, non?
Serge Gainsbourg's songs are a little naughty, aren't they?

chanter　　*to sing*
Je ne chante que sous la douche.
I only sing in the shower.

chapeau(x) m. (pl.)　　*hat*
J'ai envie de porter ce chapeau en feutre aujourd'hui.
I feel like wearing this felt hat today.

chaud(e*)*　　*hot*
Attention! La poêle est encore chaude!
Careful, the skillet is still hot!

chauffer　　*to warm, to heat up*
Si tu as faim, on peut chauffer de la soupe.
If you're hungry, we can heat up some soup.

chaussettes f. pl.　　*socks*
Elle porte rarement des chaussettes en été.
She rarely wears socks in the summer.

chemin m.　　*way, path, lane*
Le bon chemin est par là, n'est-ce pas?
This is the correct path, right?

chemin (de fer) m.　　*railroad, railway*
Mon oncle ne voyage que par chemin de fer.
My uncle only travels by rail.

chemise f.　　*shirt*
Ne me dis pas que tu vas mettre cette chemise verte-ci avec ce
pantalon rayé-là!
*Don't tell me you're going to wear this green shirt with those striped
pants!*

chemisier m.　　*blouse*
Elle a l'air très professionnel habillée en tailleur noir et chemisier
gris.
She looks very professional dressed in a black suit and a gray blouse.

cher(chère)　　*dear, expensive*
Je vous présente mon très cher ami Philippe.
Allow me to introduce my very dear friend Philip.
Ces bottes sont un peu chères, non?
These boots are rather expensive, aren't they?

chercher   *to look for*
Je suis en train de chercher un nouvel appartement parce que je
déteste mon coloc.
*I'm in the process of looking for a new apartment because I can't stand
my roommate.*

cheveu(x) m. (pl.)   *hair*
Il se brosse rarement les cheveux.
He rarely brushes his hair.

chez   *at the house or place of*
Vous dînez chez Isabelle, n'est-ce pas?
You're having dinner at Isabelle's, right?

chiffre m.   *figure, number*
Le PDG n'est pas du tout satisfait du chiffre d'affaires qu'il vient
d'annoncer.
*The CEO isn't at all satisfied with the sales figures that he just
announced.*

choisir   *to choose*
On doit choisir une destination pour notre lune de miel.
We need to choose a destination for our honeymoon.

choix m.   *choice*
Le directeur de l'établissement n'a pas eu le choix: il a exclu cet
étudiant du collège.
*The director of the school really didn't have a choice: he expelled the
student from middle school.*

chose f.   *thing*
Quelle est la chose dont tu as le plus peur?
What is the thing you're most afraid of?

ciel m.   *the sky, heaven*
Le ciel devient de plus en plus noir; il va certainement faire un
orage.
The sky is becoming increasingly darker; it's certainly going to storm.

cinéma m.   *cinema, movie theater, film*
Je fais une étude du cinéma soviétique.
I'm doing a study of Soviet cinema.

ciseaux m. pl.   *scissors*
Il ne faut pas laisser les enfants courir avec des ciseaux.
You shouldn't let children run with scissors.

clair(e)   *light, bright, clear*
L'eau dans ce lac est si claire que l'on peut voir le fond.
The water in this lake is so clear that you can see the bottom.

classe f.   *class*
Je dois aller en classe maintentant.
I have to go to class now.

clé/clef f.   *key*
Elle nous a laissé la clé sous le paillasson.
She left the key for us under the doormat.

client(e) m. (f.)   *client, customer*
Les clients de cette enterprise louche sont peu satisfaits.
The clients of this shady business are not very satisfied.

climat m.   *climate*
J'ai du mal à m'habituer au climat de ce pays.
I'm having trouble getting used to the climate of this country.

cloche f.   *bell*
On peut entendre la cloche de l'église d'ici.
We can hear the church bell from here.

cœur m.   *heart*
Je t'aime de tout mon cœur.
I love you with all my heart.

coin m.   *corner*
Notre maison est située au coin de la rue de la Fourchette et de
    l'avenue de l'Opéra.
Our house is at the corner of Fourchette Street and Opéra Avenue.

colère, en f.   *angry*
Franck est un homme désagréable qui est tout le temps en colère.
Frank is a disagreeable man who is always angry.

colis m.   *parcel, package*
Un colis vient d'arriver pour toi.
A parcel just arrived for you.

collège m.   *middle school, junior high school*
Normalement les enfants de son âge vont au college, mais
    comme Hamid est une tête il va au lycée.
*Normally kids his age go to middle school, but since Hamid is a star
    student he's going to high school.*

combien   *How much?*
Ce bouquin coûte combien?
How much does this book cost?

comme   *as, since*
Comme tu es très impoli, je ne vais pas répondre à ta question.
As you're very impolite, I'm not going to answer your question.

commencer   *to start, to begin*
Dépêche-toi! Le film commence dans dix minutes!
Hurry up! The movie starts in ten minutes!

commode   *handy, useful, convenient*
Cet outil est très commode.
This tool is very handy.

comprendre   *to understand*
J'ai du mal à comprendre son raisonnement.
I'm having a hard time understanding his reasoning.

compte m.   *account*
Avant de déménager je vais fermer mon compte en banque.
Before I move I'm going to close my bank account.

compter   *to count*
Je peux toujours compter sur Zac, c'est un mec très fiable.
I can always count on Zac; he's a really dependable guy.

conduire   *to drive*
Normalement les ados de New York ne savent pas conduire
parce qu'ils n'en ont pas besoin.
*Normally, teenagers in New York City don't know how to drive, because
they don't need to.*

confiture f.   *jam*
Cette confiture à la framboise est délicieuse.
This raspberry jam is delicious.

confondre   *to confuse, to confound*
Ce problème confond les scientifiques depuis longtemps.
This problem has confounded scientists for a long time.

confortable   *comfortable*
Notre lit n'est pas du tout confortable.
Our bed isn't comfortable at all.

conjoint(e) m. (f.)   *spouse, partner*
Mon conjoint souffre de migraines.
My spouse suffers from migraines.

connaître   *to know, to be familiar with*
Je connais beaucoup de gens qui ont ce même problème.
I know many people who have this same problem.

conseiller   *to advise, to counsel*
Notre prof vient de nous conseiller de nous inscrire à son cours
    de philo.
Our professor just advised us to enroll in his philosophy course.

consulat m.   *consulate*
Je dois récuper mon passeport au consulat avant qu'il ne ferme.
I need to pick up my passport at the consulate before it closes.

content(e)   *happy*
Je suis content de faire votre connaissance.
I am happy to meet you.

contraire   *opposite, contrary*
Tu fais toujours tout le contraire de ce que je te dis de faire.
You always do the exact opposite of what I tell you to do.

contre   *against*
Le sénateur se dit contre la nouvelle loi d'amnistie.
The senator says that he's against the new amnesty law.

copain (**copine**) m. (f.)   *friend, pal, boyfriend or girlfriend*
Ce soir il sort avec son copain Antoine.
Tonight he's going out with his friend Anthony.

corps m.   *body*
Les gens ne prennent pas assez soin de leurs corps.
People don't take good enough care of their bodies.

corriger   *to correct*
La maîtresse a besoin de corriger les interros de sa classe avant la
    fin de l'année scolaire.
*The elementary school teacher needs to correct her classs' quizzes before
    the end of the school year.*

côté m.   *side*
Le café dont on a parlé est du côté de la librairie.
The café we were talking about is on the side of the bookstore.

cou m.   *neck*
Je vais te tordre le cou!
I'm going to wring your neck!

coucher, se   *to go to bed*
Ils vont se coucher avant minuit parce qu'ils doivent se
    réveiller tôt.
They're going to bed before midnight because they have to get up early.

couleur f.   *color*
De quelle couleur est leur nouvelle voiture?
What color is their new car?

coup m.   *blow, hit*
Ces décisions prises à la hâte porteront un mauvais coup à sa
    fortune.
These hasty decisions will deal a blow to his fortune.

couper   *to cut*
Notre président a décidé de couper toute relation avec ce leader.
Our president has decided to cut all official relations with this leader.

courir   *to run*
Elle passe ses jours à courir après ses trois enfants.
She spends her days running after her three children.

courriel m.   *email*
Je viens de recevoir un courriel de mon grand-père, son premier!
I just got an email from my grandfather—his first ever!

courrier m.   *mail*
On attend toujours l'arrivée de notre courrier du jour.
We're still waiting for our daily mail delivery.

cours m.   *course, class*
Ce semestre je suis un cours de physique qui est vraiment
    ennuyeux.
This semester I'm taking a physics course that is truly boring.

court(e)   *short*
J'espère que mes cheveux pousseront parce que j'en ai marre
    d'avoir les cheveux courts.
I hope my hair grows because I'm fed up with having short hair.

couteau m.   *knife*
J'ai besoin d'un couteau pour notre partie de camping ce
    weekend.
I need a knife for our camping expedition this weekend.

coûter   *to cost*
Ces billets coûtent vraiment trop cher.
These tickets really cost too much.

crayon m.   *pencil*
Tu peux me prêter un crayon?
Can you lend me a pencil?

cri m.   *cry*
Le nouveau-né a poussé son premier petit cri du berceau.
The newborn gave its first little cry from the cradle.

croire   *to believe*
Elle ne veut pas nous croire.
She doesn't want to believe us.

cru(e)   *raw, uncooked*
Il vaut mieux manger des légumes crus autant que possible.
It's best to eat raw vegetables as much as possible

cuillère f.   *spoon*
Donne-moi une cuillère à soupe pour que je puisse manger.
Give me a soup spoon so I can eat.

cuir m.   *leather*
Malheureusement elle a décidé de porter un pantalon en cuir—
quelle horreur!
Unfortunately she decided to wear leather pants—how awful!

cuisine f.   *cuisine, type of food*
Mon père est très friand de cuisine japonaise.
My dad is quite fond of Japanese food.

cuisine, faire la   *to cook*
Aujourd'hui les jeunes n'apprennent plus à faire la cuisine.
These days young peple are no longer learning to cook.

cuisinier(-ière) m. (f.)   *cook*
Ce café a besoin de trouver un autre cuisinier porce que celui-ci
vient de démissionner.
This café needs to find another cook because this one just quit.

cuisinière f.   *cooktop, stove*
On doit remplacer notre vieille cuisinière des années 70.
We must replace our old cooktop from the '70s.

D

d'abord   *first*
D'abord on passe par la boulangerie et ensuite on ira chez le
  fleuriste.
First we are going to the bakery, and then we'll go to the flower shop.

dame f.   *lady*
Mon poème préféré de Baudelaire est "À une dame créole".
My favorite Baudelaire poem is "To a Creole Lady."

dangereux(-euse)   *dangerous*
Le hockey sur glace n'est pas aussi dangereux que le football
  américain.
Ice hockey isn't as dangerous as football.

dans   *in*
J'ai mis la nouvelle sculpture dans le salon.
I put the new sculpture in the living room.

danser   *to dance*
J'espère pouvoir danser ce soir au bal.
I hope I'm able to dance at the ball tonight.

de   *of, from*
Elle prend le train de Nantes à Paris.
She's taking the train from Nantes to Paris.

décalage horaire   *time difference, jet lag*
Comme ils souffrent du décalage horaire, ils ne vont pas pouvoir
  sortir avec nous ce soir.
*Since they're suffering from jet lag, they're not going to be able to go
  out with us tonight.*

déception f.   *disappointment*
Sa déception après la défaite était totale.
His disappointment after the defeat was complete.

décider   *to decide*
Rien n'est décidé pour le moment.
Nothing has been decided for the moment.

découper   *to cut up, to carve*
Peux-tu découper le rôti de bœuf?
Can you carve the roast beef?

décourager   *to discourage, to dishearten*
Tu nous décourages avec tous tes commentaires négatifs.
You're discouraging us with all of your negative comments.

découvrir   *to discover*
Les scientifiques espèrent découvrir une cure contre le cancer.
Scientists hope to discover a cure for cancer.

déçu(e)   *disappointed*
Je suis déçu d'apprendre ces nouvelles.
I'm disappointed to learn of this news.

dedans   *inside*
J'aime bien cette tarte parce qu'il n'y a pas de sucre dedans.
I like this tart because there isn't any sugar in it.

défendre   *to forbid*
Son père lui a défendu de fumer dans la maison.
His father forbade him from smoking in the house.

dégoût m.   *disgust*
Je ressens un sentiment de dégoût pour vos idées dangereuses.
I have a feeling of disgust for your dangerous ideas.

dehors   *outside*
Allons dehors pour prendre l'air.
Let's go outside to get some air.

déjà   *already*
J'ai déjà vu tous les films de Cédric Klapisch.
I've already seen all of Cédric Klapisch's films.

déjeuner   *to have lunch*
Tu peux déjeuner avec moi demain?
Can you have lunch with me tomorrow?

demain   *tomorrow*
Nous irons à Londres demain.
We will go to London tomorrow.

demander   *to ask*
Il nous demande de faire de notre mieux.
He's asking us to do our best.

demeurer   *to stay, to remain*
Je demeure dans cette maison jusqu'à ce qu'il me dise de partir.
I'm remaining in this house until he tells me to leave.

demi   *half*
C'est mon demi-frère.
He's my half-brother.

démodé(e)   *out of style*
Ce pantalon est vraiment démodé, tu ne devrais pas le porter.
These pants are really out of style; you shouldn't wear them.

dent f.   *tooth*
Il s'est cassé la dent en mangeant des noix.
He broke his tooth while eating nuts.

dentiste m. or f.   *dentist*
Elle poursuit des études pour devenir dentiste.
She's studying to become a dentist.

départ m.   *departure*
Téléphonez-nous avant votre départ.
Call us before your departure.

dépêcher, se   *to hurry*
Tu dois te dépêcher si tu ne veux pas manquer le train.
You should hurry if you don't want to miss your train.

dépendre de   *to depend on*
Tout cela dépend de ton effort personnel.
All of this depends on your personal effort.

dépenser   *to spend*
Quand on voyage on dépense énormément d'argent.
When you travel you spend enormous amounts of money.

depuis   *since, for how long*
Depuis combien de temps tu habites à Paris?
How long have you been living in Paris?

déranger   *to bother, to disturb*
Je ne veux pas te déranger maintenant.
I don't want to bother you now.

dernier(-ière)   *last*
Je l'ai vue la semaine dernière.
I saw her last week.

derrière   *behind*
Notre voiture est garée derrière le garage.
Our car is parked behind the garage.

des pl.　*some*
Ils veulent acheter des fleurs.
They want to buy some flowers.

dès　*from, as soon as*
Je vous contacterai dès mon retour.
I'll contact you as soon as I return.

descendre　*to come down, to go down*
Nous voulons descendre au prochain arrêt.
We want to get off at the next stop.

désirer　*to desire, to want*
Que désirez-vous?
What would you like?

dessiner　*to draw, to design*
Les enfants dessinent des animaux avec des feutres.
The kids are drawing animals with markers.

destination f.　*destination*
On aimerait un vol à destination de Nice.
We'd like a flight to Nice.

destiné(e)　*destined for, bound*
Cette chanson est destinée à devenir un grand tube sur Internet.
This song is bound to become a big hit on the Internet.

détester　*to loathe, to dislike*
Elle déteste le café, elle le trouve trop acide.
She dislikes coffee; she finds it too acidic.

devant　*in front of*
Attendons ici devant la porte.
Let's wait here in front of the door.

devenir　*to become*
Juliette veut devenir pilote.
Juliet wants to become a pilot.

devoir m.　*duty, homework*
Ce salarié n'a aucun sens du devoir professionnel.
This employee has no sense of professional duty.

devoir　*to must, to have to*
Nous allons devoir passer à la pharmacie pour acheter mes
　　médicaments.
We are going to have to stop by the pharmacy to buy my medication.

dieu m.   *God*
Les athées rejettent l'existence de Dieu.
Atheists reject the existence of God.

difficile   *difficult*
Je trouve le calcul mental vraiment difficile.
I find mental arithmetic really difficult.

dîner   *to have dinner*
On va dîner vers sept heures.
We're going to have dinner around seven.

dire   *to say*
Je n'ai rien à dire.
I don't have anything to say.

diriger   *to direct, to lead, to be in charge of*
Il dirige cette enterprise et a donc beaucoup de responsabilités.
He is in charge of this company so he has a lot of responsibilities.

distance f.   *distance*
Le sommet de la montagne est à une bonne distance d'ici.
The summit of the mountain is a good distance from here.

dizaine f.   *dozen*
Le rédacteur en chef a reçu une dizaine de lettres au sujet de
l'article diffamatoire que le journal a publié hier.
*The editor-in-chief has received a dozen letters about the slanderous
article the paper published yesterday.*

doigt m.   *finger*
Il s'est coupé le doigt en coupant une tomate.
He cut his finger while cutting a tomato.

dommage m.   *shame, pity, damage*
C'est dommage que mon fils refuse de manger des épinards.
It's a shame that my son refuses to eat spinach.

donc   *so, therefore*
Je pense, donc je suis.
I think, therefore I am.

donner   *to give*
J'espère que vous allez nous donner votre adresse.
I hope you're going to give us your address.

dormir   *to sleep*
Ma mère prend des somnifères car elle a du mal à dormir.
My mom takes sleeping pills because she has a hard time sleeping.

douane f.   *customs*
Il faut passer par la douane si vous avez quelque chose à déclarer.
You need to go to customs if you have something to declare.

douche f.   *shower*
Je prends une douche avant de me coucher.
I'm taking a shower before going to bed.

douleur f.   *pain, cramp*
Il ne peut pas supporter la douleur de sa blessure.
He can't stand the pain from his injury.

douleureux(-euse)   *painful*
Il est en train de vivre une période douleureuse de sa vie: sa
femme l'a quitté et ses enfants ne veulent plus lui parler.
*He's in the midst of a painful time in his life: his wife left him and his
kids don't want to talk to him any more.*

doute m.   *doubt*
J'ai quelques doutes à cet égard.
I have some doubts where this is concerned.

doux (-ouce)   *soft, sweet*
Cette laine est vraiment douce.
This wool is so soft.

douzaine f.   *dozen*
Donnez-moi une douzaine d'œufs s'il vous plaît.
Please give me a dozen eggs.

drapeau m.   *flag*
Combien y a-t-il d'étoiles sur le drapeau chinois?
How many stars are on the Chinese flag?

drogue f.   *drug*
Elle a besoin de drogues—c'est une toxicomane.
She needs drugs—she's an addict.

droit m.   *right, law*
Vous n'avez pas le droit de me parler ainsi.
You don't have the right to talk to me like this.

droite f.   *right*
Le café où on a mangé hier est à droite.
The café where we ate yesterday is on the right.

dur(e)   *hard, difficult, harsh*
L'étudiant passe un examen très dur.
The student is taking a very difficult exam.

E

eau f.   *water*
Je ne bois que de l'eau minérale plate.
I only drink flat mineral water.

échanger   *to exchange*
Sophie passe par le magasin de chaussures pour échanger les sandales qu'elle a achetées l'autre jour.
Sophie is stopping by the shoe store to exchange the sandals she bought the other day.

école f.   *school*
Il vient de trouver un poste dans une école près d'ici.
He just got a job at a nearby school.

écolo m., f.   *(colloquial) "green," environmentally friendly, environmentalist*
Les écolos manifestent contre cette usine qui pollue nos fleuves.
The environmentalists are protesting against this factory that pollutes our rivers.

économe   *thrifty*
Si tu étais plus économe, tu n'aurais pas tous ces problèmes d'argent.
If you were more thrifty, you wouldn't have all of these money problems.

écouter   *to listen to*
Le soir nous aimons écouter du jazz à la radio.
At night we like to listen to jazz on the radio.

écrire   *to write*
Si vous n'aimez pas cet article, vous devez écrire une lettre à la rédaction.
If you don't like this article, you should write a letter to the editor.

écriteau m.   *post, sign*
L'écriteau dit "Défense de Fumer", donc tu devrais éteindre ta cigarette.
The sign says "No Smoking," so you should put out your cigarette.

effet m.   *effect*
On sait très bien l'effet que cette loi va avoir sur les chômeurs.
We know very well the effect that this law is going to have on the unemployed.

égal(e) *equal, the same*
Ça m'est égal.
It's all the same to me.

égalité f. *equality*
La devise de la France est "Liberté, Égalité, Fraternité."
France's motto is "Liberty, Equality, Fraternity."

église f. *church*
Ça fait trois ans que je n'ai pas mis les pieds dans une église.
It's been three years since I've set foot in a church.

elle f. *she*
Elle est charmante, n'est-ce pas?
She's quite charming, isn't she?

embassade f. *embassy*
L'Ambassade américaine est juste en face de ce bâtiment.
The American embassy is just across the street from this building.

embrasser *to kiss, to embrace*
J'ai envie de t'embrasser.
I feel like kissing you.

emploi m. *job*
Si tu as besoin d'un emploi, cherche dans les petites annonces.
If you need a job, look in the want ads.

employé(e) *employee*
Les employés de ce bureau sont tous nuls!
The employees in this office are all worthless!

enchanté(e) *delighted, enchanted*
Je suis enchanté de faire votre connaissance.
I am delighted to meet you.

encore *more, still*
Voulez-vous encore du pain?
Would you like more bread?

encre m. *ink*
J'ai besoin d'acheter des cartouches d'encre pour mon stylo.
I need to buy some ink cartridges for my pen.

endroit m. *place, spot*
Quel bel endroit!
What a beautiful spot!

enfant m.   *child*

Ce pauvre enfant n'a plus de famille, il est orphelin.
This poor child doesn't have any family; he's an orphan.

ennui m.   *problem, boredom*

Je pense que tu vas avoir des ennuis avec ton coloc si tu ne paies
pas les factures ce mois-ci.
*I think your're going to have problems with your roommate if you don't
pay the bills this month.*

ennuyer   *to bother, to annoy*

Pourquoi tu veux m'ennuyer avec ce genre de question?
Why do you want to bother me with this type of question?

enseigner   *to teach*

Madame Garnier est capable d'enseigner le grec, le latin et
l'italien.
Madame Garnier is able to teach Greek, Latin, and Italian.

ensemble   *together*

Allons ensemble au spectacle.
Let's go together to the show.

ensuite   *next, after, then*

D'abord nous avons vu un nouveau film qui vient de sortir et
ensuite nous avons pris un pot au bar.
First we saw a new film that just came out, then we had a drink at the bar.

entendre   *to hear*

Tu entends ce bruit à l'extérieur? Qu'est-ce que c'est?
Do you hear this noise outside? What is it?

entendu, bien   *of course*

Elle invitera toutes ses amies à la fête, bien entendu.
She will, of course, invite all of her friends to the party.

entre   *between*

Vous trouverez l'aire de jeux entre la librairie et le musée.
You'll find the playground between the bookstore and the museum.

entrée f.   *entrance, admission*

Où est la porte d'entrée?
Where is the entrance?

entrer   *to enter*

Elle est entrée par la porte de derrière.
She came in through the back door.

envie de, avoir   *to feel like doing something*
Elle a envie de passer trois semaines au bord de la mer.
She feels like spending three weeks at the seaside.

envoyer   *to send*
Je dois acheter des timbres pour envoyer une lettre en Italie.
I need to buy stamps to send a letter to Italy.

épaule f.   *shoulder*
Il s'est fait mal à l'épaule.
He hurt his shoulder.

épicé(e)   *spicy*
La cuisine de ce pays est un peu trop épicée pour moi.
The food from this country is a bit too spicy for me.

équipe f.   *team*
Elle aime bien travailler en équipe.
She likes teamwork.

escale f.   *stopover*
Je préfère un vol sans escale, si possible.
I prefer a flight without stopovers, if possible.

escalier m.   *stairs*
J'ai peur des escaliers en colimaçon, je n'en prends jamais.
I am afraid of spiral staircases; I never take them.

espace m.   *space*
Il y a beaucoup d'espace dans cet apartment.
There is a lot of space in this apartment.

espagnol   *Spanish*
Elle parle espagnol couramment.
She speaks Spanish fluently.

espèces f.   *cash*
Ce restaurant n'accepte pas les cartes de crédit; il faut payer en
espèces.
This restaurant does not accept credit cards; you must pay in cash.

espérer   *to hope*
Ils espèrent aller au Maroc cet été.
They hope to go to Morocco this summer.

essayer   *to try*
Nous essayons de finir notre travail avant le début du match.
We're trying to finish our work before the beginning of the game.

essence f.   *gasoline, petrol*
L'essence coûte plus cher en France qu'aux États-Unis.
Gasoline costs more in France than in the United States.

et   *and*
Caroline a acheté des carottes, des poivrons et de la salade au
    marché.
Caroline bought carrots, peppers, and lettuce at the market.

étage m.   *floor*
Notre appartement est au troisième étage.
Our apartment is on the third floor.

état m.   *state*
Le chef d'État est ici en visite officielle.
The Head of State is here on an official visit.

États-Unis m. pl.   *the United States*
Barack Obama est le quarante-quatrième président des
    États-Unis.
Barack Obama is the forty-fourth president of the United States.

étoile f.   *star*
L'étoile du nord est très facile à repérer.
The North Star is very easy to find.

étrange   *strange, odd*
Je trouve ses propos étranges, et toi?
I find his words strange, do you?

étranger(-ère)   *foreigner, stranger*
Pour visiter notre pays, les étrangers auront désormais besoin
    d'un visa spécial.
*In order to visit our country, foreigners will from now on need a special
    visa.*

être   *to be*
Elle désire être psychiatre.
She would like to be a psychiatrist.

étudiant(e) m. f.   *student*
Elle est étudiante à la fac.
She is a student at the university.

étudier   *to study*
Tu dois étudier sérieusement si tu veux réussir à l'examen.
You should study seriously if you want to pass the exam.

eux m.   *them*
  Je pense à eux quand je visiste cet endroit.
  I think about them when I visit this place.

examen m.   *exam, test*
  Notre examen de physique était presque impossible!
  Our physics test was practically impossible!

excursion f.   *excursion, trip, outing*
  Les écoliers attendent avec impatience leur excursion au zoo.
  The school children are impatiently waiting for their outing to the zoo.

expérience f.   *experience; experiment*
  Je n'ai pas beaucoup d'expérience dans ce domaine.
  I don't have a lot of experience in this area.
  Les scientifiques montent une grande expérience au labo.
  The scientists are starting a big experiment in this lab

expliquer   *to explain*
  Tu devrais lui expliquer pourquoi tu ne veux plus le voir.
  You should explain to him why you don't want to see him any more.

F

fabriquer   *to make*
  Dans cette usine on fabrique des appareils photo numériques.
  In this factory they make digital cameras.

face (en...de)   *in front of, across*
  Mon bureau est en face du parc municipal.
  My office is across from the municipal park.

fâcher, se   *to become angry*
  Ne dis pas cela à Margaux, elle se fâche facilement.
  Don't tell that to Margot; she gets angry quite easily.

facile   *easy*
  L'interrogation était assez facile mais l'élève ne l'a a tout de
     même pas réussie.
  The quiz was easy enough but the student still didn't pass it.

facture f.   *bill, invoice*
  Je viens de recevoir ma facture et on s'est trompé sur le montant
     à payer.
  *I just received my invoice, and they made an error in the amount to be
     paid.*

faim m.   *hunger*
Donne-lui à manger parce qu'il a faim.
Give him something to eat because he's hungry.

faire   *to do, to make*
Il songe à faire une tarte pour la fête ce soir.
He's thinking about making a pie for the party tonight.

famille f.   *family*
Ma famille et moi pensons venir vous rendre visite.
My family and I are thinking about coming to visit you.

fatigué(e)   *tired*
Cette nuit je n'ai pas fermé l'œil donc je suis fatigué ce matin.
Last night I didn't get a wink of sleep, so I am tired this morning.

faut, il (que)   *It is necessary that*
Il faut que ayons plus de patience avec elle, elle est très troublée.
It is necessary that we have more patience with her—she is quite troubled.

faute f.   *fault*
Ce n'est pas de ma faute!
It's not my fault!

félicitations f. pl.   *Congratulations*
Félicitations! On vient de voir les photos de ton nouveau-né.
Congratulations! We just saw the pictures of your newborn.

femme f.   *woman, wife*
La femme d'à côté est une musicienne très talentueuse.
The woman next door is a very talented musician.

fenêtre f.   *window*
On a besoin de remplacer les fenêtres pour que notre maison soit mieux isolée.
We need to replace our windows so that our house is better insulated.

fermé(e)   *closed*
La bibliothèque de notre village est fermée le weekend.
Our village's library is closed on weekends.

fermer   *to close*
Fermez la porte! Il y a des courants d'air.
Close the door! There's a draft.

fête f.   *party*
Je ne peux pas assister à la fête ce soir parce que j'ai trop de travail.
I can't come to the party tonight because I have too much work.

feu m. *fire*
Le bâtiment abandonné a pris feu hier soir.
The abandoned building caught on fire last night.

fièvre f. *fever*
Cet enfant a une fièvre élevée—emmenez-le à la salle des urgences.
This child has a high fever—take him to the emergency room.

figure f. *face*
Elle se lave la figure avant de se coucher.
She washes her face before going to bed.

fil, un coup de m. *phone call*
Passez-nous un coup de fil quand vous serez prête à partir.
Give us a phone call when you're ready to leave.

fille f. *girl, daughter*
Après trois fils, ils sont très heureux d'avoir une fille.
After three sons, they are very happy to have a girl.

fils m. *son*
J'ai deux filles et un fils.
I have two daughters and a son.

fin f. *end*
Quelle est la fin de l'histoire?
What's the end of the story?

finir *to finish*
Je dois finir mon travail avant de sortir.
I have to finish my work before going out.

fleur f. *flower*
Quelle est ta fleur préférée? Moi j'aime bien les tulipes.
What's your favorite flower? Personally, I like tulips.

fleuve m. *river*
Le Nil est le plus long fleuve du monde.
The Nile is the longest river in the world.

flic m. *(colloquial) cop*
Après quelques minutes, les flics sont finalement arrivés sur la scène de l'accident.
After a few minutes, the cops finally arrived at the scene of the accident.

fois f.   *time, times*
Combien de fois as-tu visité Montréal?
How many times have you visited Montréal?
Soccer is a worldwide sport, whereas American football is liked only in the United States.

forfait m.   *fixed-price, package deal*
Il vaut mieux acheter le forfait parce que tout est compris.
It's better to buy the package deal because everything is included.

forme f.   *figure, shape*
Après deux ans de yoga intensif, elles sont en très bonne forme.
After two years of intensive yoga, they're in very good shape.

fort(e)   *strong*
Même s'il n'est pas très musclé il est tout de même très fort.
Even if he's not very muscular, he's still quite strong.

fourchette f.   *fork*
Mets la fourchette à côté de la cuillière.
Put the fork next to the spoon.

frais(-aîche)   *cool, fresh*
Il fait frais ici le matin mais il commence à faire plus chaud vers midi.
It's cool here in the morning, but it starts to get warmer around noon.

français m.   *French*
Je parle français et un peu espagnol aussi.
I speak French and a little Spanish, too.

Français(e) m. f.   *French*
Il s'est marié avec une Française.
He married a Frenchwoman.

francophone   *French-speaking*
Voilà la première fois que je visite un pays francophone.
This is the first time I am visiting a French-speaking country.

frapper   *to hit, to knock*
Ecoute—j'entends quelqu'un frapper à la porte!
Listen—I hear someone knocking on the door!

frites f. pl.   *French fries*
J'essaie de ne plus manger de frites, elles sont très mauvaises pour la santé.
I'm trying to no longer eat French fries as they are very bad for your health.

froid(e)   *cold*

Il fait très froid à Montréal en hiver.
It's very cold in Montreal in the winter.

front m.   *forehead, front*

Les ouvriers veulent organiser un front politique.
The workers want to organize a political front.

frontière f.   *border*

La frontière entre la France et l'Italie est très facile à passer.
The border between France and Italy is very easy to cross.

fumer   *to smoke*

Il n'est pas facile pour mon père de cesser de fumer après trente ans.
It's not easy for my father to quit smoking after thirty years.

G

gai(e)   *happy, gay*

Quelle est cette chanson gaie que tu fredonnes?
What is this happy song you're humming?

gai   *gay, homosexual*

Didier lutte pour le mariage gai.
Didier is fighting for gay marriage.

gant m.   *glove*

Cela me va comme un gant.
It fits me like a glove.

garçon m.   *boy*

Ce jeune garçon est caractériel, il n'écoute jamais sa mère.
This young boy is a troublemaker; he never listens to his mother.

gare f.   *train station*

Peut-on prendre un taxi pour aller à la gare?
Can we take a cab to go to the train station?

gare routière f.   *bus station*

La gare routière est à cinq minutes d'ici.
The bus station is five minutes from here.

garer   *to park*

J'ai horreur de garer cette grande voiture en ville.
I hate parking this big car in the city.

gauche   *left*
Dans certains pays, il ne faut jamais serrer la main avec la main gauche.
In some countries you should never shake with the left hand.

genou(x) m. (pl.)   *knee(s)*
Suite à sa chute, l'athlète a mal aux genoux.
After his fall, the athlete's knees hurt.

genre m.   *sort, type, kind*
Quel genre de fromage aimes-tu?
What type of cheese do you like?

gens m. pl.   *people*
Il ne faut pas faire attention à ce que disent les gens que tu ne connais pas.
You shouldn't pay attention to what is said by people you don't know.

gentil(le)   *nice, kind*
Notre nouveau prof est intelligent mais pas très gentil.
Our new teacher is smart but not very nice.

gérant(e)   *manager*
Je vous présente la nouvelle gérante de nos affaires, Madame Lemtouni.
Let me intoduce you to our new business manager, Mrs. Lemtouni.

gîte m.   *shelter, rental cottage*
On a trouvé un gîte dans le Limousin pour un très bon prix sur Internet.
We found a rental cottage in the Limousin region for a really good price on the Internet.

glace f.   *ice, ice cream, mirror*
Veux-tu de la glace au chocolat?
Would you like some chocolate ice cream?
On voit notre image dans la glace.
We can see our reflection in the mirror.

gorge f.   *throat*
J'ai mal à la gorge.
My throat hurts.

goûter   *to taste*
J'aime bien goûter tous ces fromages de votre région.
I really like tasting all these cheeses from your region.

goûter m.   *afternoon snack*
Mes enfants prennent du pain avec du fromage comme goûter.
My kids have bread with cheese for an afternoon snack.

grand(e)   *big, large*
Ce bateau a la plus grande voile que j'ai jamais vue.
This boat has the biggest sail I've ever seen.

grand magasin m.   *department store*
Au lieu d'acheter en ligne, je préfère fréquenter les grands
   magasins.
Instead of shopping online I prefer going to department stores.

gris(e)   *gray*
Tu es très beau dans ton costume gris; mets-le pour ton entretien
   d'embauche.
You are really handsome in your gray suit; wear it for your job interview.

gros(se)   *fat*
Ce gros oiseau est si drôle!
This fat bird is so funny!

guerre f.   *war*
Ces deux pays sont constamment en guerre l'un avec l'autre.
These two countries are constantly at war with each other.

guichet m.   *ticket office*
Elle nous a dit de récupérer nos billets au guichet.
She told us to pick up our tickets at the ticket office.

guide m.   *guide, guidebook*
Le guide nous a montré plein de sites intéressants.
The guide showed us many interesting sites.

H

habiller, s'   *to get dressed*
Je dois m'habiller pour aller à l fête.
I need to get dressed to go to the party.

habiter   *to live, to dwell*
Vincent habite dans la deuxième maison à gauche.
Vincent lives in the second house on the left.

haïr   *to hate*
J'ai ne comprends pas les gens qui haïssent les chats.
I don't understand people who hate cats.

handicappé(e) *handicapped, disabled*
Il n'y a aucun accès aux handicappés à ce bâtiment.
There is no handicapped access to this building.

haut(e) *high, tall*
Ce bâtiment n'est pas très haut.
This building isn't very tall.

haut, en *above, upstairs*
Notre chambre est en haut.
Our bedroom is upstairs.

heure f. *hour, time*
Quelle heure est-il?
What time is it?

heureux(-euse) *happy*
Elle très heureuse de pouvoir finalement visiter la Suède.
She's very happy to finally be able to visit Sweden.

hier *yesterday*
On est allé au café hier, mais c'était fermé.
We went to the café yesterday, but it was closed.

homme m. *man*
Je trouve que l'homme là-bas ressemble beaucoup à mon frère.
I think that the man over there looks a lot like my brother.

homme/femme d'affaires *businessman/woman*
J'ai remarqué que les hommes d'affaires sont tous très attachés à
leur portable.
I've noticed that businessmen are all really attached to their cellphones.

horaire m. *timetable, schedule*
Il me faut un horaire récent.
I need a current timetable.

horreur f. *horror, monstrosity*
Elle porte des sandales vertes avec des chaussettes jaunes? Quelle
horreur!
She's wearing green sandals with yellow socks? What a monstrosity!

hors (de) *out, outside*
Ceci est hors de question!
This is out of the question!

hôtel m. *hotel*
On a réservé une chambre dans un hôtel très chic.
We reserved a room in a really swanky hotel.

hôtel de ville m.   *city hall, town hall*
   Ils vont se marier à l'Hôtel de Ville.
   They're getting married at city hall.

I

ici   *here*
   J'habite ici depuis 1975.
   I've lived here since 1975.

idée (f)   *idea*
   Quelle idée novatrice!
   What an innovative idea!

il   *he*
   Il est souvent drôle mais très sérieux aussi.
   He's often funny but also very serious.

il y a   *there is, there are*
   Il y a trop de monde ici.
   There are too many people here.

ils(elles) m. (pl.)   *they*
   Ils sont tellement inintelligibles que je comprends très peu de ce
      qu'ils disent.
   They are so unintelligible that I understand very little of what they say.

immédiatement   *immediately*
   Rendez-moi mon argent immédiatement.
   Give me back my money immediately.

immeuble m.   *building*
   Notre immeuble est très bien situé.
   Our building has a great location.

immigré(e) m. (f.)   *immigrant*
   Il y a beacoup d'immigrés qui sont récemment venus dans ce
      pays.
   Many immigrants have recently come to this country.

imperméable m.   *raincoat*
   Mets ton imperéeable parce qu'il va certainement pleuvoir ce
      matin.
   Put your raincoat on because it'll certainly rain this morning.

impoli(e)   *impolite*
   Elle est si impolie que je refuse de l'inviter à notre fête.
   She is so rude that I refuse to invite her to our party.

importer   *to import*
Le Mexique importe de plus en plus de produits d'autres pays d'Amérique latine.
Mexico is importing more and more products from other Latin American countries.

impôt m.   *tax*
La société pour laquelle je travaille est obligée de payer plus d'impôts cette année.
The company that I work for is obligated to pay more taxes this year.

impuissant(e)   *powerless, helpless; impotent*
Je me sens impuissant face à mes peurs.
I feel powerless when faced with my fears.

indiquer   *to point out, to indicate*
Tu peux m'indiquer le site dont tu me parlais?
Can you point out the website you were telling me about?

infirmier(-ière) m. (f.)   *nurse*
Les infirmiers de cet hôpital menacent de faire une grève si les conditions de travail ne s'améliorent pas bientôt.
The nurses in this hospital are threatening to go on strike if work conditions don't improve soon.

information f.   *piece of information*
Ils ont une information qui risque de t'intéresser.
They have a piece of information that might interest you.

informatique f.   *computer science*
Je suis en informatique pour l'instant, mais je vais probablement changer de spécialisation.
I'm in computer science now but I'm probably going to change majors.

inquiet(-ète)   *worried*
Comme on n' a pas de nouvelles, on est très inquiet.
As we haven't had any news, we're quite worried.

inquiétude f.   *worry, concerns*
Vos actions suscitent des inquiétudes parmi vos collègues.
Your actions are causing worries among your colleagues.

interdit(e)   *forbidden, off limits*
Cette boîte est interdite aux mineurs.
This nightclub is off limits to minors.

intéressant(e)   *interesting; attractive*
C'est un philosophe qui a écrit beaucoup de livres intéressants.
He's a philosopher who has written many interesting books.
Le prix de cet appareil-photo est très intéressant.
The price of this camera is quite attractive.

inutile   *useless, pointless*
Inutile de leur dire de nous téléphoner, ils ne le feront jamais.
It's pointless telling them to call us—they'll never do it.

invité(e) m. f.   *guest*
Dépêche-toi parce que les invités arrivent dans trois quarts d'heure.
Hurry up because the guests are arriving in forty-five minutes.

inviter   *to invite*
Le couple a invité 150 personnes à son mariage.
The couple invited one hundred and fifty people to their wedding.

J

jadis   *in the past, in the old days*
Jadis les enfants aimaient bien ce jeu.
In the past children liked this game.

jamais   *ever*
As-tu jamais visité Nantes? C'est une ville extraordinaire.
Have you ever visited Nantes? It's an extraordinary city.

jamais, ne   *never*
Je ne mange jamais de viande parce que je suis végétalien.
I never eat meat because I'm vegan.

jambe f.   *leg*
Elle est tombée dans l'escalier et s'est fait mal à la jambe.
She fell on the stairs and hurt her leg.

jardin m.   *garden*
Cet été-là on a passé énormément de temps ensemble dans son jardin.
That summer we spent an enormous amount of time together in her garden.

jaune   *yellow*
Celui qui gagne l'étape du jour du Tour de France a le droit de porter le maillot jaune.
Whoever wins the day's stage of the Tour de France has the right to wear the yellow jersey.

je *I*
Je suis ravi de faire votre connaissance.
I'm thrilled to meet you.

jeter *to throw, to throw out*
Il faut jeter les déchets dans la poubelle.
Throw the trash in the garbage can.

jeu m. *game, match*
Eh bien, il faut jouer le jeu si tu veux réussir.
Well, you have to play the game if you want to get ahead.

jeune *young*
Bonjour, jeune homme!
Hello, young man!

joie f. *joy*
Quelle joie de te revoir après toutes ces années!
What a joy to see you again after all these years!

joindre *to connect*
Il est bon de joindre l'utile à l'agréable.
It is good to connect the useful with the pleasant.

joli(e) *pretty*
Il nous a offert un joli petit cadeau.
They gave us a lovely little present.

jouer *to play*
Tu joues de la guitaire? Moi aussi!
You play the guitar? Me, too!

jouet m. *toy*
Il y a trop de jouets par terre dans ta chambre!
There are too many toys on the floor in your room!

jour m. *day*
Nos invités seront là dans trois jours.
Our guests will be here in three days.

journal m. *newspaper*
De plus en plus de gens lisent le journal sur Internet.
More and more people are reading the news on the Internet.

journée f. *day*
On a passé une journée très agréable au bord de la mer.
We spent a really nice day by the seaside.

juger   *to judge*
On a du mal à juger la situation.
We're having a hard time judging the situation.

jupe f.   *skirt*
Ma fille a acheté cette jupe à Paris l'été dernier.
My daughter bought this skirt in Paris last summer.

jusqu'à   *until, up to*
On sera à Bordeaux jusqu'à la fin du mois.
We'll be in Bordeaux until the end of the month

K

kif-kif   *(colloquial) all the same*
Tu préfères du soda ou du citron pressé? Kif-kif! J'aime bien les deux.
Do you prefer soda or lemonade? It's all the same to me! I like both of them.

kilomètre m.   *kilometer*
Notre maison est à quinze kilomètres d'ici.
Our house is fifteen kilometers from here.

klaxonner   *to honk the horn*
Il est interdit de klaxonner dans certaines villes.
It is forbidden to honk the horn in certain cities.

L

la   *the, it, her*
La maison n'est pas loin d'ici.
The house isn't far from here.
La pomme? Je vais la manger.
The apple? I'm going to eat it.
On la connaît, elle est très drôle.
We know her; she's very funny.

là   *here, there*
Anne, t'es où? Je suis là!
Anne, where are you? I'm here!

lac m.   *lake*
Cet été on va faire du canotage sur le lac.
This summer we're going to go canoeing at the lake.

laid(e)   *ugly*
Moi je trouve cette robe vraiment laide.
Personally, I think this dress is really ugly.

laisser   *to leave*
Je veux passer par la maison pour y laisser mes affaires.
I want to stop by the house and leave my things there.

langue f.   *language, tongue*
Quelle est ta langue maternelle?
What is your native language?
Elle s'est brûlé la langue en buvant du thé chaud.
She burnt her tongue drinking hot tea.

laquelle(lesquelles) f. pl.   *which one(s)*
Laquelle tu préfères—la verte ou l'orange?
Which one do you prefer—the green one or the orange one?

lard m.   *bacon*
Je prends des œufs au lard, et toi?
I'm having eggs and bacon, and you?

large   *broad, wide*
Au sens large du terme, on dirait qu'elle est libérale.
In the broadest sense of the term, you could say that she is liberal.

larme f.   *tear*
Larmes aux yeux, l'enfant a rendu le petit chatton qu'elle avait trouvé à son voisin.
Tears in her eyes, the child gave the kitten she'd found back to her neighbor.

laver   *to wash*
J'espère qu'ils vont laver leur voiture avant de partir en vacances.
I hope they're going to wash their car before going away on vacation.

laver, se   *to wash oneself*
Le gamin doit se laver avant de se coucher.
The child needs to wash before going to bed.

le   *the, it, him*
Je prends le métro pour aller à mon bureau.
I take the metro to go to work.
Mon manuel de physique? Je ne le veux plus. Vends-le!
My physics textbook? I don't want it any more. Sell it!
Je vais le voir demain.
I'm going to see him tomorrow.

leçon f.　　*lesson*
　　Le prof n'a rien préparé pour la leçon d'aujourd'hui.
　　The teacher didn't prepare anything for today's lesson.

lecteur DVD m.　　*dvd player*
　　Elle ne peut pas regarder ce film parce que notre lecteur DVD est
　　en panne.
　　She can't watch the film because our dvd player is broken.

lentement　　*slowly*
　　Conduis plus lentement, s'il te plaît!
　　Drive more slowly, please.

lequel(lesquels) m. pl.　　*which one(s)*
　　J'aime bien ce pantalon. Lequel?
　　I really like this pair of pants. Which one?

les　　*the, them*
　　Les chats sont aussi intelligents que les chiens. Moi, je les déteste
　　tous.
　　Cats are as smart as dogs. I hate them all.

lettre f.　　*letter*
　　Il a reçu une lettre qui l'a complètement bouleversé.
　　He received a letter that has completely upset him.

leur　　*their, to them*
　　Vous avez leur argent?
　　Do you have their money?
　　Je leur ai parlé hier.
　　I spoke to them yesterday

lever　　*to raise*
　　Levez la main si vous voulez parler.
　　Raise your hand if you wish to speak.

lever, se　　*to get up*
　　Je me couche tôt parce que demain je dois me lever à 6h.
　　I'm going to bed early because tomorrow I have to get up at 6 a.m.

libre　　*free, available*
　　Cette place est libre?
　　Is this seat free?

ligne f.　　*line*
　　Prenez la ligne orange pour aller au centre-ville.
　　Take the orange line to go downtown.

lire   *to read*
Il se plaint parce qu'il n'a pas assez de temps pour lire ce qu'il veut.
He's complaining because he doesn't have enough time to read what he wants.

lit m.   *bed*
On vient d'acheter un lit pour notre fils.
We just bought a bed for our son.

litre m.   *liter*
Donnez-moi un litre de cidre, s'il vous plaît.
Give me a liter of cider, please.

livre m.   *book*
Les jeunes d'aujourd'hui achètent peu de livres.
Today's youth buy few books.

location f.   *renting out, rental*
On cherche une agence de location.
We're looking for a rental agency.

logiciel m.   *software*
Mon frère a développé un logiciel qui fait du traitement de texte.
My brother developed a software program that does word processing.

loi f.   *law*
Le sénateur dit qu'il va voter contre cette loi ridicule.
The senator says that he'll vote against this absurd law.

loin   *far*
Notre voiture est garée un peu loin d'ici.
Our car is parked a bit far from here.

lointain   *distant, remote*
Elle vient d'un village bien lointain.
She comes from a very remote village.

louer   *to rent*
On aimerait bien louer un appartement dans le centre-ville.
We'd like to rent an apartment downtown.

lui   *him, him/her*
C'est qui? C'est lui.
Who is it? It's he.
Je lui parle au téléphone au moins trois fois par jour.
I talk to him/her at least three times a day.

lumière f. *light*
Quand nous étions jeunes, mon frère avait une lumière
stroboscopique dans sa chambre.
When we were young, my brother had a strobe light in his room.

lune f. *moon*
J'aime contempler la lune.
I love to contemplate the moon.

lunettes f. pl. *eyeglasses*
Je ne peux rien voir sans mes lunettes.
I can't see anything without my glasses.

M

madame f. *Mrs., lady*
Madame Meunier travaille ici depuis vingt ans.
Mrs. Meunier has worked here for thirty years.

mademoiselle f. *Miss*
Mademoiselle, je peux vous aider?
Miss, may I help you?

magasin m. *store, shop*
Il y a plein de magasins dans ce quartier.
There are many stores in this neighborhood.

main f. *hand*
Il s'est brûlé la main en versant du café.
He burned his hand pouring coffee.

maintenant *now*
Maintenant il y a très peu d'étudiants qui n'ont pas d'ordinateur.
Now there are very few students who don't have a computer.

mairie f. *town hall*
Ils se sont d'abord mariés à la mairie et puis à l'église.
They got married first at the town hall and then at church.

mais *but*
J'aimerais faire une tarte Tatin mais je n'ai pas de pommes.
I'd like to make a Tatin tart but I don't have any apples.

maison f. *house*
Ils sont en train d'acheter leur première maison.
They are in the process of buying their first house.

maître(-esse) m. (f.)   *elementary school teacher, owner*
Le maître essaie de calmer ses élèves avant l'épreuve.
The teacher is trying to calm his student before the test.
Qui est le maître de ce chien perdu?
Who is the owner of this lost dog?

mal   *badly*
Elle danse bien mais chante très mal.
She dances well but sings very badly.

malade   *sick*
Comme elle est malade, elle ne peut pas voyager.
Since she's sick she can't travel.

malentendu m.   *misunderstanding*
Rien n'est pareil entre eux depuis le grand malentendu de l'été dernier.
Nothing is the same between them since the big misunderstanding of last summer.

malgré   *in spite of, despite*
Malgré tous nos problèmes de transport, nos vacances étaient magnifiques.
In spite of all our transportation problems, our vacation was fantastic.

malheur m.   *misfortune, adversity, tragedy*
J'ai le malheur de vous dire que votre cours est annulé.
I have the misfortune of telling you that your class is canceled.

malice m.   *mischief, malice*
C'est un homme plein de malice qui aime faire souffrir les autres.
He's a man who is full of malice and likes to make others suffer.

malicieux(-euse)   *mischievous*
Cet enfant malicieux est très drôle, mais il cause des problèmes à l'école.
This mischievous child is very funny, but he causes problems at school.

manger   *to eat*
On va manger vers midi.
We're going to eat around noon.

manière f.   *manner, way*
La manière dont vous me parlez est inacceptable.
The way in which you're speaking to me is unacceptable.

manquer   *to miss, to lose*
Tu me manques.
I miss you.
On vient de manquer le train du 14h45.
We just missed the 2:45 train.

manteau m.   *coat*
Mets ton manteau parce qu'il va faire très frais ce matin.
Put on your coat because it's going to be chilly this morning.

marché m.   *market, open-air market*
Elle est passée par le marché en plein air pour acheter des fruits.
She stopped by the open-air market to buy some fruit.

marcher   *to walk*
Après son accident, il a du mal à marcher.
After his accident, he has a hard time walking.

mari m.   *husband*
Son mari est assez désagréable.
Her husband is somewhat disagreeable.

mariage m.   *marriage*
Cet enfant est né du premier mariage de mon frère.
This child is from my brother's first marriage.

massif(-ive)   *massive, huge*
Les géologues ont trouvé un rocher massif lors de leur fouille.
The geologists discovered a massive rock while on their dig.

mauvais(e)   *bad, wrong*
Quelle mauvaise idée!
What a bad idea!
On a pris le mauvais chemin.
We took the wrong way.

me   *me, to me*
Il va me donner les clés.
He's going to give me the keys.
Elle me regarde.
She's looking at me.

médecin m.   *doctor*
Je dois voir le médecin car je me sens très malade.
I need to see the doctor because I feel really sick.

médicament m.   *medication*
Elle a besoin de ce médicament pour combattre son infection.
She needs this medication to fight her infection.

meilleur(e)   *better*
Je trouve que cet hôtel est bien meilleur que l'autre.
I think this hotel is much better than the other one.

même   *even, same*
Tu as le même problème que moi; tu es fauché!
You have the same problem as me—you're broke!

mensonge m.   *lie*
Le candidat ne fait que dire des mensonges.
The candidate is only telling lies.

mer f.   *sea*
Notre hôtel est près de la mer.
Our hotel is near the sea.

merci   *thanks*
On dit "merci" quand on reçoit un cadeau.
One says "thanks" when receiving a present.

mériter   *to deserve*
C'est une employée qui ne mérite aucune augmentation de
   salaire; elle est nulle!
She's an employee who doesn't deserve a raise at all; she's a loser!

mètre m.   *meter*
L'arrêt de bus est à 200 mètres d'ici.
The bus stop is 200 meters from here.

métro m.   *subway*
On a pris le métro pour aller à Montmartre.
We took the subway to go to Montmartre.

mets m. pl.   *dishes, delicacies*
On a assisté à un dîner où on a goûté des douzaines de mets
   internationaux.
We went to a dinner where we sampled dozens of international dishes.

mettre   *to put, to place, to wear*
Tu peux mettre ces fleurs dans un vase?
Can you put these flowers in a vase?
Tu mets quoi pour la fête?
What are you wearing to the party?

meubles f. pl.   *furniture*
J'espère remplacer toutes ces meubles vétustes.
I hope to replace all of this outdated furniture.

Midi, le m.   *the South of France*
Elle va visiter le Midi cet été.
She going to visit the South of France this summer.

mien(-enne) m. (f.)   *mine*
Ce livre est à toi? Oui, c'est le mien.
Is this book yours? Yes, it's mine.
C'est à qui, cette jupe? C'est la mienne.
Whose skirt is this? It's mine.

mieux   *better*
Il chante beaucoup mieux que moi; je n'ai pas l'oreille musicale.
He sings much better than I do; I don't have a musical ear.

mille m.   *thousand*
Tu me dois mille dollars, tu sais.
You owe me a thousand dollars, you know.

minuit m.   *midnight*
Cendrillon a dû rentrer chez elle avant minuit.
Cinderella needed to be home before midnight.

misère f.   *poverty, destitution*
Malheureusement, beaucoup de familles vivent dans la misère.
Unfortunately, a lot of families live in poverty.

mode f.   *style, fashion*
Ces gants ne sont plus à la mode.
These gloves are no longer in style.

moi m.   *me, the self*
Donnez-moi une idée de ce que vous voulez.
Give me an idea of what you want.
Elle écrit une thèse sur de thème du moi dans l'art romantique.
She's writing a thesis on the theme of the self in Romantic art.

moindre, le/la   *the least*
Ça, c'est le moindre de tes problèmes!
That's the least of your problems!

moins, de   *less*
Elles ont beaucoup moins d'espace que nous.
They have a lot less space than we do.

mois m.   *month*
On viendra chez vous le mois prochain.
We'll come to your place next month.

moitié, la f.   *half of*
Il ne reste que la moitié du travail à faire.
Only half of the work remains to be done.

moment m.   *moment, time, a while*
Ça va prendre un bon moment, tu sais.
It's going to take a while, you know.

mon, (ma, mes) m. (f., pl.)   *my*
Mon ami est très comique.
My friend is really funny.
Ma mère habite en Islande.
My mother lives in Iceland.
Je vais rendre visite à mes amis espagnols à Barcelone.
I'm going to visit my Spanish friends in Barcelona.

monde m.   *world*
Le monde est si vaste.
The world is so huge.

monnaie f.   *currency, change*
Est-ce que je peux faire de la monnaie, s'il vous plaît?
Can I get some change, please?

Monsieur m.   *mister, sir*
Monsieur, je peux vous aider?
Sir, may I help you?

montagne f.   *mountain*
Ils vont à la montagne pour faire du ski.
They're going to go skiing in the mountains.

monter   *to go up, to take something up*
Ok, je vais monter.
Ok, I'm going upstairs.
Tu peux monter la lessive?
Can you take the laundry up?

montre f.   *watch*
Comme cadeau, elle espère acheter une montre suisse à son
     oncle.
She hopes to buy her uncle a Swiss watch for a gift.

montrer   *to show*
Pouvez-vous nous montrer cette montre-ci?
Can you show us this watch?

morceau m.   *a piece of*
Tu veux un morceau de gâteau?
Do you want a piece of cake?

mort(e)   *dead*
Notre chatton est mort ce matin d'une maladie mystérieuse.
Our kitten died this morning from a mysterious illness.

mosquée f.   *mosque*
J'admire l'architecture de cette mosquée médiévale.
I admire the architecture of this medieval mosque.

mot m.   *word*
Je ne connais pas ce mot.
I don't know this word.

moto f.   *motorcycle*
Il est venu à pied? Non, à moto.
Did he come on foot? No, he came by motorcycle.

mouchoir m.   *handkerchief, tissue*
Donne-moi un mouchoir pour que je puisse me moucher.
Give me a tissue so I can blow my nose.

mourir   *to die*
Le soldat a révélé au journaliste qu'il a peur de mourir sur le
champ de bataille.
*The soldier admitted to the journalist that he's afraid of dying on the
battlefield.*

moyen m.   *means, way*
Par quel moyen espérez-vous le convaincre?
By what means do you hope to convince him?

moyen(-ne)   *medium*
Elle est de taille moyenne.
She's medium sized.

mur m.   *wall*
Les ouvriers recontruisent le mur qui a été détruit par l'orage.
The workers are rebuilding the wall that was destroyed by the storm.

musée m.   *museum*
Notre ville vient d'ouvrir un musée municipal qui contient une grande collection.
Our city just opened a muncipal museum that houses a huge collection.

musique f.   *music*
Elle apprécie toutes sortes de musique.
She appreciates all types of music.

N

nager   *to swim*
Si vous aimez nager, allez à la piscine près d'ici, elle est très agréable.
If you like to swim, go to the pool near here; it's quite nice.

navette f.   *shuttle*
Je prendrai la navette de l'aéroport à l'hôtel.
I will take the shuttle from the airport to the hotel.

né(e), être   *to be born*
Je suis né à Dakar en 1965.
I was born in Dakar in 1965.

ne . . . ni . . . ni   *neither . . . nor*
Je n'ai ni frère ni sœur.
I have neither a sister nor a brother.

nécessaire   *necessary*
Il est nécessaire que tu fasses un plus grand effort.
It's necessary that you make a greater effort.

neige f.   *snow*
J'aime bien la neige mais j'ai horreur du froid.
I like the snow but I hate the cold.

nerfs m. pl.   *nerves*
Qu'est-ce qu'il me tape sur les nerfs!
Oh, how he grates on my nerves!

nerveux(-euse)   *nervous*
Elle devient très nerveuse avant de parler à ses profs.
She becomes quite nervous before speaking to her teachers.

nettoyer   *to clean*
Vous devez nettoyer la salle de bain avant l'arrivée des invités.
You need to clean the bathroom before the guests arrive.

nez m. *nose*
Elle est très jolie malgré son nez retroussé.
She's quite pretty despite her snub nose.

noël m. *Christmas*
Joyeux Noël!
Merry Christmas!

noir(e) *black*
Je vais mettre un pull noir avec un jean délavé.
I'm going to wear a black sweater with stone-washed jeans.

noix f. pl. *nuts, walnuts*
Ma cousine est allergique à toutes sortes de noix.
My cousin is allergic to all kinds of nuts.

nom m. *name*
Quel est votre nom?
What is your name?

nombre m. *number*
Il y a un très grand nombre d'étudiants qui veut étudier en
     France.
There is a great number of students who want to study in France.

non *no*
Tu peux me prêter de l'argent? Non, non et non!
Can you lend me some money? No, no, and no!

normal(e) *normal*
Il n'est pas normal que tu ne manges qu'une fois par jour.
It's not normal that you only eat once a day.

notre(nos) m. or f. (pl.) *our*
Notre chien aboie constamment quand il est en laisse! Nos
     voisins doivent nous détester!
Our dog constantly barks on the leash! Our neighbors must hate us!

nourriture f. *food*
Mes enfants adorent la nourriture japonaise.
My kids love Japanese food.

nous *we, us,*
Nous voudrions vous téléphoner. Vous pouvez nous donner
     votre numéro de téléphone?
We would like to call you. Can you give us your phone number?

nouveau(-elle)   *new*
Je vous présente mon nouveau coloc, Jean-Pierre.
Let me introduce my new roommate, Jean-Pierre.
Avez-vous une nouvelle adresse?
Do you have a new address?

nouvelles f. pl.   *news*
As-tu appris les nouvelles? Paul et Virginie divorcent.
Have you heard the news? Paul and Virginia are getting divorced.

nuage m.   *cloud*
Il y a beaucoup de nuages dans le ciel, va-t-il faire un orage?
There are a lot of clouds in the sky; is it going to storm?

nuit f.   *night*
Je ne sors jamais la nuit.
I never go out at night.

nuitée f.   *overnight stay*
On a payé trois nuitées mais comme l'hôtel était désagréable, on
    est parti après deux jours.
*We paid for three overnight stays but since the hotel was unpleasant, we
    left after two days.*

nul(-le)   *hopeless, worthless, invalid*
Ce film est nul!
This movie is worthless!

numéro m.   *number*
Quel est ton numéro de portable?
What's your cellphone number?

O

obéir   *to obey*
Il faut obéir aux lois du pays, sinon on risque de se faire arrêter.
One must obey the laws of the land; if not one risks being arrested.

objet m.   *object*
Cet objet sert à quoi?
What is this object for?

obtenir   *to obtain, to get*
Mon fils espère obtenir son permis de conduire cet été.
My son is hoping to get his driver's license this summer.

occasion f.   *event, opportunity*
  Notre visite nous donne l'occasion de voir un ami qui habite ici
    depuis longtemps.
  *Our visit is giving us the opportunity to see a friend who has lived here
    for a long time.*

occupé(e)   *busy*
  Je suis très occupé en ce moment.
  I'm very busy at the moment.

œil(yeux) m. (pl.)   *eye*
  Mon oncle a un œil de verre et une jambe de bois.
  My uncle has a glass eye and a wooden leg.

œuf m.   *egg*
  Normalement le matin je prends un œuf à la coque.
  In the morning I usually have a soft-boiled egg.

œuvre f.   *work of art, body of work*
  J'ai lu toutes les œuvres de Zola; c'est mon écrivain préféré.
  I've read Zola's body of work; he's my favorite writer.

oiseau(æ) m. (pl.)   *bird*
  Il n'y a rien de plus agréable que le chant des oiseaux que l'on
    entend chez nous le matin.
  *There's nothing more beautiful than the morning birdsong that we hear
    at our house.*

ombre f.   *shadow, shade*
  Tu dois mettre ton bébé à l'ombre; le soleil est très fort
    aujourd'hui.
  You should put your baby in the shade; the sun is really strong today.

ordinateur m.   *computer*
  Elle a acheté un nouvel ordinateur en ligne.
  She bought a new computer online.

ordonnance f.   *prescription*
  Est-ce que j'ai besoin d'une ordonnance pour avoir ces gouttes?
  Do I need a prescription to get these drops?

oreille f.   *ear*
  Elle a trois piercings à l'oreille.
  She has three piercings in her ear.

oreiller m.   *pillow*
  Je préfère dormir sans oreiller.
  I prefer to sleep without a pillow.

os m.   *bone*
Notre chien aime bien ronger les os.
Our dog loves to gnaw on bones.

ou   *or*
Qu'est-ce que tu aimes mieux—les chats ou les chiens?
Which do you prefer, cats or dogs?

où   *where*
Tu vas où?
Where are you going?

oublier   *to forget*
Elle a tendance à oublier ses clés chez moi.
She has a tendency to forget her keys at my place.

oui   *yes*
Vous parlez français? Oui, bien sûr.
Do you speak French? Yes, of course.

ouvert(e)   *open*
Le musée sera ouvert de midi à minuit.
The museum will be open from noon to midnight.

ouvrage m.   *work, book*
Un nouvel ouvrage de mon poète préféré vient de paraître il y a
    quelques semaines.
A new book by my favorite poet was just published a few weeks ago.

ouvrir   *to open*
Elle rêve d'ouvrir un petit restaurant dans cet immeuble.
She dreams of opening a small restaurant in this building.

P

PACS m.   *"pacte civil de solidarité" (civil union in France)*
Les partenaires liés par PACS bénéficient de nombreux droits.
Partners who are joined in a PACS are entitled to numerous rights.

pain m.   *bread*
Il est essentiel de servir ce plateau de fromage avec beaucoup de
    pain.
It's vital to serve this cheese plate with a lot of bread.

palais m.   *palace*
Les touristes ont envie de voir le palais royal.
The tourists are eager to see the royal palace.

pantalon m. *pants*
Il a acheté un pantalon bleu.
He bought a pair of blue pants.

papier m. *paper*
Donne-moi du papier pour mon imprimante.
Give me some paper for my printer.

par *by*
Elle est passée par le marché en rentrant.
She stopped by the market on her way home.

paraît que, il *It appears that*
Il paraît que les enfants aiment bien ce film.
It appears that kids love this film.

paraître *to appear, to show*
Il ne laisse rien paraître de ses sentiments.
He doesn't let his feelings show at all.

parapluie m. *umbrella*
Prends ton parapluie parce qu'il va certainement pleuvoir
 aujourd'hui.
Take your umbrella because it's certainly going to rain today.

parc m. *park*
Ce printemps on espère visiter quelques parcs nationaux et faire
 du camping.
This spring we hope to visit a few parks and do some camping.

parce que *because*
Je l'aime bien parce qu'elle est généreuse.
I like her because she's generous.

pardonner *to excuse, to forgive*
Il faut le pardonner, il ne sait pas ce qu'il dit.
You must excuse him; he doesn't know what he's saying.

parent(e) *relative, relation, parent*
Je suis parent avec elle.
I am her relative.

parfois *sometimes*
Parfois je me balade dans mon jardin quand je m'ennuie.
Sometimes I go for a stroll in my garden when I am bored.

parler *to speak, talk*
Je dois te parler.
I need to talk to you.

parmi   *among*
Il semble toujours y avoir de la mauvaise herbe parmi les fleurs.
There always seem to be weeds among the flowers.

parole f.   *speech, word, promise*
J'aime bien cette chanson mais j'ai oublié les paroles.
I like this song but I've forgotten the words.

partie f.   *part*
La meilleure partie de ce film est la fin—tout explose!
The best part of this movie is the end—everything explodes!

partout   *all over, everywhere*
Elles ont voyagé ensemble partout en Europe.
They traveled together all over Europe.

pas   *negation*
Elle (n')a pas faim.
She isn't hungry.
Note: *The (ne) of the negation is rarely pronounced in spoken French.*

pas m.   *step*
Tu fais un pas en arrière.
You are taking a step back.

passer   *to spend, to pass, to stop by*
On va passer quelques semaines en Tunisie.
We're going to spend a few weeks in Tunisia.

pauvre   *poor*
La famille de mon mari est très pauvre donc ils vont venir habiter
   chez nous.
My husband's family is quite poor so they're going to come live with us.

pays m.   *land, country*
Vous êtes de quel pays?
What country are you from?

paysage m.   *landscape*
Les artistes aiment bien venir ici pour dessiner ce paysage serein.
Artists like to come here to draw this tranquil landscape.

PDG   *CEO*
Je viens de faire la connaissance de notre nouveau PDG; il a l'air
   très gentil.
I just met our new CEO; he seems very nice.

peau f.   *skin*
La peau du visage de mon oncle est ridée.
The skin on my uncle's face is wrinkled.

peindre   *to paint*
Elle a suffisament d'argent pour peindre sa maison, mais elle ne
     veut pas le faire.
She has enough money to paint her house, but she doesn't want to do it.

peine f.   *sorrow, grief*
Il a beaucoup de peine en ce moment.
He has a lot of sorrow at the moment.

peine, à   *hardly*
On était à la fête depuis à peine dix minutes quand on a reçu un
     coup de fil de notre babysitter nous demandant de renter.
*We had hardly been at the party for ten minutes when we got a call
     from our babysitter asking us to come home.*

pendant   *during*
Elle a pleuré pendant toute la pièce de théâtre.
She cried during the entire play.

penser   *to think*
Qu'est-ce que tu penses de la situation actuelle?
What do you think about the current situation?

perdre   *to lose*
Notre équipe va certainement perdre ce soir.
Our team is certainly going to lose tonight.

permettre   *to permit, to enable*
Ce nouveau logiciel va vous permettre de vite calculer vos
     impôts.
This new software will enable you to quickly calculate your taxes.

personne   *no one, nobody*
Personne ne demande l'impossible.
No one asks the impossible.

petit(e)   *small, little*
On a un petit problème.
We have a small problem.

peu, un   *a few, a bit*
Tu as soif? Oui, un peu.
Are you thirsty? Yes, a bit.

peur, avoir *to be afraid*
L'enfant a peur des serpents.
The child is afraid of snakes.

peut-être *maybe, perhaps*
Il y a peut-être près de 3 000 SDF dans cette ville.
The are perhaps close to 3,000 homeless people in this city.

phrase f. *sentence*
Le maître a écrit la phrase au tableau.
The teacher wrote the sentence on the board.

pièce f. *room*
Combien de pièces y-a-t-il dans cet appartement?
How many rooms are there in this apartment?

pied m. *foot*
J'ai mal au pied.
My foot hurts.

pierre f. *rock*
Que celui qui n'a jamais péché lui jette la première pierre.
Let he who is without blame cast the first stone.

piéton m. *pedestrian*
Les piétons ne peuvent pas traverser la rue parce qu'il y a trop de circulation.
The pedestrians can't cross the street because there is too much traffic.

piloter *to drive, to pilot*
Il a piloté sa voiture à une vitesse de plus de 125 km/heure.
He drove his car at a speed of over 125 km an hour.

pilule f. *pill, the Pill*
Elle prend la pilule depuis deux ans.
She's been taking the Pill for two years.

piscine f. *swimming pool*
On a fait construire une piscine chez mes parents.
We had a swimming pool built at my parents' house.

pittoresque *picturesque*
Ce petit village est très pittoresque.
This little village is quite picturesque.

place f. *place, seat, square*
Cette place est résérvée.
This seat is reserved.

plafond m. *ceiling*
Le plafond de verre n'est pas un mythe, c'est vrai!
The glass ceiling isn't a myth, it's true!

plage f. *beach*
Les enfants pourraient passer des semaines entières à la plage si leurs mères le permettaient.
Children would spent entire weeks at the beach if their mothers let them.

plaisanterie f. *joke*
Ne te fâche pas—c'était une plaisanterie!
Don't get mad—it was a joke!

plaisir m. *pleasure*
Quel plaisir de vous voir!
What a pleasure to see you!

plancher m. *floor*
Je ne sais pas comment nettoyer ce plancher en céramique.
I don't know how to clean this tile floor.

plat m. *dish*
Ce restaurant sert de très bons plats végétariens.
This restaurant serves very good vegetarian dishes.

plat(e) *flat*
Je trouve ce paysage plat un peu déprimant.
I find this flat landscape a bit depressing.

plein(e) *full*
Le plein, s'il vous plaît!
Fill 'er up, please!

pleurer *to cry*
L'enfant ne cesse jamais de pleurer, j'en peux plus!
The kid never stops crying—I can't take it anymore!

pleuvoir *to rain*
Selon les prévisions météo, il va pleuvoir toute la journée.
According to the weather forecast, it's going to rain all day.

pluie f. *rain*
Cette pluie m'embête.
This rain is getting to me.

plupart (de) *most, majority*
La plupart des Parisiens n'ont pas de voiture.
The majority of Parisians don't have a car.

plus   *more*
Il y a plus de choix dans ce magasin que dans l'autre.
There are more choices in this store than in the other one.

plusieurs   *several*
Il y a plusieurs films qui m'intéressent en ce moment.
There are several films that interest me at the moment.

plutôt   *rather, somewhat*
Les cheveux de ma fille sont plutôt ondulés.
My daughter's hair is rather wavy.

poche f.   *pocket*
Mets tes clés dans ta poche.
Put your keys in your pocket.

poids m.   *weight*
Il a perdu du poids récemment.
He lost weight recently.

point m.   *point*
Choisissons un point de rencontre.
Let's choose a meeting point.

poli(e)   *polite*
C'est un homme très poli.
He's a very polite man.

police f.   *police*
Certains résidents de cette ville ont peur de la police.
Certain residents of this city are afraid of the police.

polluer   *to pollute*
Cette entreprise doit payer une amende car elle a pollué ce lac
   pendant dix ans.
*This company has to pay a fine because it polluted this lake for ten
   years.*

pont m.   *bridge*
Ce pont relie les deux parties du village.
This bridge connects the two parts of the village.

port m.   *port*
Marseille est le port le plus actif de France.
Marseille is the most active port in France.

portable m.   *cellphone, laptop*
Donne-moi ton portable pour que je puisse donner un coup de fil
  à Vincent.
Give me your cellphone so I can call Vincent.
J'emporte mon portable en vacances, comme ça je peux écrire
  mon roman.
I'm bringing my laptop on vacation so I can write my novel.

porte f.   *door*
Entrons par la porte de devant.
Let's go in by the front door.

portefeuille m.   *wallet*
Elle a offert un portefeuille en cuir à son père pour son
  anniversaire.
She gave her father a leather wallet for his birthday.

porter   *to wear, to carry*
Il va porter un nouveau costume pour son entretien demain.
He's going to wear a new suit for his interview tomorrow.
Les passagers portent leurs bagages à bord.
The passengers are carrying their bags on board.

poste m.   *position, job*
Il a trouvé un poste au Québec avec une enterprise internationale.
He found a job in Québec with an international company.

poste f.   *post office*
On peut acheter des timbres à la poste.
We can buy stamps at the post office.

pour   *for*
Tiens, le facteur a apporté une lettre pour toi.
Here you go, the letter carrier brought you a letter.

pourboire m.   *tip*
Les serveurs se plaignent des clients radins qui laissent des
  mauvais pourboires.
The waiters are complaining about cheap customers who leave bad tips.

pourquoi   *why*
Pourquoi es-tu si triste? Qu'est-ce qu'il y a?
Why are you so sad? What's wrong?

pouvoir   *to be able to*
Pouvez-vous me téléphoner?
Are you able to call me?

prendre   *to take, to have*
Ils vont prendre un vol de Montréal à Ottawa.
They're taking a flight from Montreal to Ottawa.
Elle prend son café en écoutant la radio.
She has her coffee while listening to the radio.

près de   *near*
On cherche une maison près du parc.
We're looking for a house near the park.

presque   *almost*
Mes ancêtres habitent dans cette région depuis presque cent ans.
My ancestors have lived in this region for almost a hundred years.

pressé(e)   *in a hurry*
Le directeur ne peut pas nous parler parce qu'il est pressé.
The director can't talk to us because he's in a hurry.

prêter   *to lend*
Je refuse de vous prêter de l'argent.
I refuse to lend you money.

prix m.   *price*
Quel est le prix de ces billets?
What is the price of these tickets?

prochain(e)   *next*
On se verra l'année prochaine.
We'll see each other next year.

prof m.   *teacher, professor*
On a été très surpris de découvrir que notre prof de philo déteste lire!
We were very surprised to find out that our philosophy professor hates to read!

projet m.   *project*
Nous attendons le financement pour notre projet.
We are waiting for the financing for our project.

promenade f.   *walk*
Faisons une promenade!
Let's take a walk!

promener, se   *to go on a walk*
Ils veulent se promener pour prendre l'air.
They want to go on a walk to get some fresh air.

propre *clean*
La chambre de mon fils est toujours très propre.
My son's room is always very clean.

propriétaire m. or f. *owner*
Nous voulons contacter le propriétaire de ce terrain pour
l'interviewer.
We want to contact the owner of this land to interview him.

protéger *to protect*
On dit que cette loi va protéger les animaux en voie de
disparition.
It is said that this law is going to protect endangered animals.

publicité f. *advertisement*
Je déteste cette chaîne, il y a toujours trop de publicités.
I hate this channel—there are always too many advertisements.

puis *then*
D'abord je suis allé au pressing et puis chez le fleuriste.
First I went to the dry cleaner's, and then to the flower shop.

Q

quai m. *quay, pier, platform*
Les voyageurs attendent le train sur le quai.
The travelers are waiting for their train on the platform.

quand *when*
Quand devez-vous partir?
When do you have to leave?

quant à *as for, as far as . . . is concerned*
Quant à lui, je pense qu'il a eu tort d'avoir réagi d'une telle
manière.
*As far as he is concerned, I think that he was wrong to have reacted in
such a manner.*

quartier m. *neighborhood*
Ce quartier est si délabré que je ne veux plus y vivre.
This neighborhood is so dilapidated that I don't want to live here any more.

que *what, that*
Le film que nous avons vu était ridicule.
The film that we saw was ridiculous.
Que voulez-vous dire?
What do you mean?

quelque chose *something*
Il a quelque chose pour toi.
He has something for you.

quelque part *somewhere*
Mon portable doit être ici quelque part.
My cellphone should be here somewhere.

quelqu'un *someone*
Quelqu'un t'appelle.
Someone is calling you.

qui *who, whom*
Qui voulez-vous voir?
Whom do you wish to see?
Notre enterprise cherche quelqu'un qui puisse faire la
 comptabilité.
Our business is searching for someone who can do accounting.

quitter *to leave*
On aimerait bien quitter cette ville, mais comment?
We'd love to leave this city, but how?

quoi *what*
Tu veux que je fasse quoi?
You want me to do what?

R

raconter *to tell, to recount*
Racontez-nous l'histoire de votre voyage à Tanger.
Tell us the story of your trip to Tangiers.

raison f. *reason*
Voici la raison pour laquelle je ne te parle plus: tu es trop égoïste!
Here's the reason why I don't talk to you any more—you're so selfish!

raison, avoir *to be right*
Vous avez complètement raison.
You are totally right.

randonnée f. *hike, hiking*
Faisons une randonnée après le déjeuner.
Let's take a hike after lunch.

ranger   *to put away, to put into order*
Rangez vos jouets ou vous resterez à l'intérieur pour le reste de l'après-midi!
Put your toys away, or you'll stay inside for the rest of the afternoon!

rapide   *fast*
Voilà le train le plus rapide du monde.
Here's the fastest train in the world.

rappeler   *to remind*
Pouvez-vous me rappeler votre nom?
Can you remind me of your name?

rebours, à   *backwards*
Le gamin compte à rebours.
The child is counting backwards.

recette f.   *recipe*
Ma mère faisait des petits gâteaux délicieux, mais j'ai perdu la recette.
My mother made delcious cookies, but I've lost the recipe.

recevoir   *to receive, to get*
Elle espère recevoir beaucoup de cadeaux pour son anniversaire.
She hopes to get a lot of gifts for her birthday.

reconnaître   *to recognize*
Ta barbe est si longue que l'on ne te reconnaît plus!
Your beard is so long that we no longer recognize you!

reçu m.   *receipt*
J'ai perdu un reçu dont j'ai besoin pour mon travail.
I lost a receipt that I need for my work.

rédaction f.   *writing, essay, composition*
La rédaction est à rendre le 23 mai.
The composition is due May 23rd.

regarder   *to watch*
Tu veux regarder un film avec moi?
Do you want to watch a movie with me?

régime m.   *regime, diet*
Il suit un régime pour perdre du poids.
He's on a diet to lose weight.

règle f.   *rule*
Les règles de sécurité sont faciles à suivre.
The safety regulations are easy to follow.

regretter   *to regret, to feel sorry*
Ils regrettent que tu sois si triste.
They feel sorry that you are so sad.

reine f.   *queen*
Elle se déguise en reine pour la fête.
She's dressing up as a queen for the party.

remercier   *to thank*
Je vous remercie.
Thank you.

remettre   *to put back, to hand back, to hand over*
Elle m'a remis la lettre sans rien dire.
She handed me the letter without saying anything.

remplir   *to fill*
Elle a rempli le seau avec de l'eau.
She filled the bucket with water.

rencontre f.   *meeting, meet-up, encounter*
Elle nous parle de sa rencontre avec un cinéaste très connu.
*She's telling us about her encounter with a very well-known film
    director.*

rencontrer   *to meet*
J'ai rencontré beaucoup de collègues au congrès.
I met a lot of colleagues at the conference.

rendre   *to give back, to render or make*
Le prof va rendre les rédactions demain.
The teacher is going to give back the compostions tomorrow.
Ça me rend heureux.
That makes me happy.

rendre visite   *to visit someone*
Mes cousins vont nous rendre visite l'été prochain.
My cousins are going to visit us next summer.

repas m.   *meal*
Comme elle est malade, elle prend ses repas au lit.
Since she's sick, she has her meals in bed.

répéter   *to repeat*
Elle ne fait que répéter ce que les autres disent.
She only repeats what others say.

répondre   *to answer, to respond*
Comment a-t-il répondu à ta question?
How did he answer your question?

respirer   *to breathe*
Le yoga m'apprend à respirer.
Yoga teaches me to breathe.

rester   *to stay*
Tu restes ici pendant combien de semaines?
How many weeks are you staying here?

résumer   *to sum up, to summarize*
Je vais résumer pour toi en un mot: viré!
I'm going to sum it up for you in one word: fired!

retard, en   *late*
Ils arriveront en retard, comme toujours.
They'll arrive late, as usual.

retirer   *to withdraw, to pull out*
Elle retire de l'argent de la banque pour payer ses factures.
She's withdrawing money from the bank to pay her bills.

retour m.   *return*
Votre retour est pour quand?
When are you returning?

réussir   *to succeed, to pass (an exam)*
Votre fils est un étudiant brillant qui résusssira dans la vie.
Your son is a brilliant student who will succeed in life.

réunion f.   *meeting*
Notre réunion est pour 14h.
Our meeting is at 2 pm.

réveiller, se   *to wake up*
Normalement je me réveille vers sept heures du matin.
Normally I get up around seven a.m.

revenir   *to come back*
Tu reviens quand?
When are you coming back?

rêver   *to dream*
Hier soir j'ai rêvé que je passais des vacances en Egypte.
Last night I dreamed that I was on vacation in Egypt.

revue f.   *magazine*
J'ai lu un très bon article dans cette revue.
I read a very good article in this magazine.

rhume m.   *cold*
J'ai un rhume depuis lundi.
I've had a cold since Monday.

riche   *riche*
Ce couple est riche mais a très mauvais goût.
This couple is rich but has very bad taste.

rien   *nothing*
Rien n'est impossible.
Nothing is impossible.

rire   *to laugh*
C'est un homme qui adore rire.
He's a man who loves to laugh.

robe f.   *dress*
Quelle jolie robe, tu l'as achetée où?
What a beautiful dress; where did you buy it?

roi m.   *king*
Le roi vient de mourir. Vive la reine!
The king has died. Long live the queen!

rôti m.   *roast*
On va servir des légumes avec notre rôti.
We're going to serve vegetables with our roast.

rouge   *red*
Il a brûlé le feu rouge et a eu une amende.
He ran a red light and got a ticket.

route f.   *way, highway, road, route*
Connaissez-vous la route qui mène à cette ville?
Do you know the road that leads to this city?

rue f.   *street*
Les enfants de ce quartier aiment jouer dans la rue.
Kids in this neighborhood like to play in the street.

S

sale   *dirty*
Je refuse de monter dans sa voiture parce qu'elle est trop sale.
I refuse to ride in his car because it's too dirty.

salé(e)   *salty*
J'adore les frites parce qu'elles sont salées.
I love French fries because they are salty.

salle à manger f.   *dining room*
On va déjeuner dans la salle à manger.
We're going to have lunch in the dining room.

salle de bain f.   *bathroom*
Elle a de l'eau de Javel pour nettoyer sa salle de bain.
She has some bleach for cleaning her bathroom.

salon m.   *living room*
Prenons du thé dans le salon.
Let's have some tea in the livingroom.

saluer   *to greet*
Il faut apprendre aux étudiants comment saluer les gens dans
    d'autres pays.
It's necessary to teach students how to greet people in other countries.

salut   *hi*
Salut Pierre! Salut Miriam, ça va?
Hi, Peter! Hi, Miriam! How are you?

sang m.   *blood*
Il y a eu un accident dans la rue et il y a du sang partout.
There was an accident in the street, and there is blood everywhere.

sans   *without*
Je ne peux pas fonctionner sans café.
I can't function without coffee.

santé f.   *health*
Elle est en bonne santé.
She's in good health.

sauf   *except, but*
Il travaille tous les jours sauf le lundi.
He works every day but Monday.

sauter *to jump; to leave out, skip*

Hier j'ai vu les mômes de mon quartier sauter à la corde, elles sont très talentueuses!

Yesterday I saw the neighborhood kids jumping rope—they are really talented!

Tu n'as pas besoin de lire tout ce document, saute jusqu'à la fin.

You don't need to read the whole document; skip to the end.

savoir *to know*

Nous voudrions savoir si elle sait nager.

We would like to know if she can swim.

savon m. *soap*

Elle fabrique du savon avec ses enfants.

She makes soap with her kids.

se *oneself*

Il se lave.

He's washing himself

sec(-èche) *dry*

Je voudrais un martini sec.

I'd like a dry martini.

sécher *to dry*

Tu devrais faire sécher ton maillot de bain au soleil.

You should dry your swimsuit in the sun.

second(e) *second, second-rate*

C'est un hôtel de seconde classe.

It's a second-rate hotel.

secours m. *help*

Au secours!

Help!

sel m. *salt*

Mets du sel dans la sauce, elle est un peu fade.

Put some salt in the sauce; it's a bit bland.

selon *according to*

Selon les experts, les changements s'effectueront tout de suite.

According to the experts, the changes will take place immediately.

semaine f. *week*

On s'est vus la semaine dernière.

We saw each other last week.

siècle m.   *century*
Elle étudie la musique du dix-neuvième siècle.
She is studying nineteenth-century music.

signer   *to sign*
Pouvez-vous signer ici, s'il vout plaît?
Can you sign here, please?

soie f.   *silk*
Elle portait une robe en soie magnifique.
She wore a magnificent silk dress.

soif, avoir f.   *to be thirsty*
Avez-vous soif?
Are you thirsty?

soir m.   *night, evening*
Il fait assez chaud le soir dans cette région.
It's pretty warm in this region in the evenings.

soirée f.   *night, evening*
On a passé une soirée agréable avec nos amis.
We spent a pleasant evening with our friends.

soleil m.   *sun*
Le soleil brille très fort.
The sun is shining brightly.

son (sa, ses) m. (f., pl.)   *hers / his*
J'aime son fils / sa fille / ses enfants.
I like his / her son / his / her daughter / his / her kids.

souci m.   *problem, worry*
Il a beaucoup de soucis en ce moment avec son travail.
He has a lot of problems at work these days.

soudainement   *suddenly*
On n'avait pas vu Eric pendant des mois et puis soudainement il
    nous a contacté.
We hadn't seen Eric for months and then suddenly he contacted us.

souffrance f.   *suffering*
Elle a connu beaucoup de souffrances dans sa vie.
She's experienced a lot of suffering in her life.

souhait m.   *desire, wish*
Mon souhait le plus cher est de revoir mes amis en Irelande.
My fondest wish is to see my friends in Ireland again.

souhaiter   *to wish/hope for, to desire*
Il est à souhaiter que tout le monde accepte ces changements.
It is to be hoped that everyone will accept these changes.

souper m.   *dinner (Québec)*
Tu prends quoi comme souper?
What are you having for dinner?

souper   *to have dinner (Québec)*
Ce soir on va souper chez Caroline.
Tonight we're having dinner at Caroline's.

sourire   *to smile*
Elle sourit tout le temps.
She smiles all the time.

sous   *under, beneath*
Si je ne suis pas là, glisse le contrat sous ma porte.
If I'm not there, slide the contract under my door.

souvenir, se (de)   *to remember*
Je me souviens de toi!
I remember you!

souvent   *frequent*
On dîne souvent dans ce restaurant, on y mange très bien.
We frequently have dinner in this restaurant—the food is really good.

spectacle m.   *show*
J'ai assisté à un spectacle hier soir qui était formidable.
I went to a show last night that was fantastic.

stationner   *to park*
Il est interdit de stationner devant cette porte.
Parking in front of this door is forbidden.

stylo m.   *pen*
Le prof exige que ses élèves utilisent un stylo à encre.
The teacher requires that her students use a fountain pen.

sucre m. *sugar*
Tu prends du sucre avec ton thé?
Do you take sugar with your tea?

sucré(e)   *sweet*
Je n'aime pas la confiture; c'est trop sucrée.
I don't like jam; it's too sweet.

suivant(e)   *next, following*
On prendra le train suivant.
We'll take the next train.

suivre   *to follow, to take (a course)*
Je ne peux pas suivre votre argument.
I can't follow your argument.
Elles suivent un cours d'allemand.
They're taking a German course.

sujet de, au   *about*
Il rédige un article au sujet de la violence à l'école.
He's writing an article about violence in schools.

sur   *on*
Le stylo est sur la table, n'est-ce pas?
The pen is on the table, right?

sûr(e)   *sure, reliable, certain*
Je suis sûre que tu vas aimer cette chanson!
I'm sure you're going to love this song!

surtout   *above all*
J'aime bien le vin blanc mais j'aime surtout le vin rouge.
I like white wine, but I like red wine above all.

surveiller   *to put under surveillance, to watch, to supervise*
J'évite le sucre parce que je surveille mon poids.
I avoid sugar because I'm watching my weight.

T

tabac m.   *tobacco, tobacco shop*
Je suis allergique à la fumée de tabac.
I'm allergic to tobacco smoke.

table f.   *table*
Mettons-nous à table.
Let's sit down at the table.

tableau(x) m. (pl.)   *picture, painting*
Cet après-midi on a vu des tableaux magnifiques.
This afternoon we saw some magnificent paintings.

taille f.   *size*
Il est de taille moyenne.
He's medium-sized.

tasse f.   *cup*
Voulez-vous une tasse de thé?
Would you like a cup of tea?

taux m.   *level, rate*
Quel est le taux de change aujourd'hui?
What's the exchange rate today?

te   *you, to you*
Je t'aime.
I love you.
Il va t'écrire plus tard.
He's going to write to you later.

tel(le)   *such*
Un tel comportement va te causer des problèmes avec ton patron.
Such behavior is going to cause you problems with your boss.

télécharger   *to download*
Elles téléchargent des documents pour leur présentation cet
après-midi.
They are downloading documents for their presentation this afternoon.

téléphoner   *to call, to phone*
Il va nous téléphoner quand il aura fini.
He's going to call us when he's finished.

tellement   *so much, so*
Je suis tellement content de vous voir.
I'm so happy to see you.

tempête f.   *storm*
Les enfants espèrent que l'école sera fermer à cause de la
tempête.
The kids are hoping that the school will close due to the storm.

temps m.   *time, weather*
Je n'ai pas le temps de te parler.
I don't have time to talk to you.
Quel temps fera-t-il demain?
What will the weather be tomorrow?

tenir   *to hold*
Tu dois me tenir la main quand on traverse cette rue.
You need to hold my hand when we cross this busy street.

terre f.   *land, earth*
L'agriculteur a besoin de cultiver sa terre avant la prochaine saison.
The farmer needs to cultivate his land before the next season.

tête f.   *head*
Elle veut des comprimés parce qu'elle a mal à la tête.
She wants some pills because she has a headache.

thé m.   *tea*
Et si on prenait une tasse de thé?
How about having a cup of tea?

timbre f.   *stamp*
Combien de timbres faut-il pour une lettre internationale?
How many stamps are needed for an international letter?

tissu m.   *fabric, material*
Il me faut du tissu pour la robe que je fais en ce moment.
I need fabric for the dress I'm making now.

toi   *you*
Elle est plus âgée que toi.
She's older than you.

toilette, faire sa f.   *to wash, to do one's daily hygiene routine*
Elle fait sa toilette avant de s'habiller.
She washes before getting dressed.

tomber   *to fall*
L'enfant doit faire attention, sinon il va tomber.
The child needs to be careful or else he'll fall.

ton(ta, tes) m. (f., pl.)   *your*
J'aime ton pull / ta chemise / tes sabots.
I like your sweater / your shirt / your clogs.

ton m.   *tone*
Je n'apprécie pas le ton de ce message.
I don't appreciate the tone of this message.

tôt   *early*
Couche-toi maintenant parce qu'on se lève tôt demain.
Go to bed because we're getting up early tomorrow.

toucher   *to touch, to reach, to affect*
Regardez, mais ne touchez pas à mes affaires!
Look, but don't touch my things!
Le tabagisme touche tout le monde.
Tobacco addiction affects everyone.

toujours   *always*
Elle a toujours un sourire pour ses étudiants.
She always has a smile for her students.

tour f.   *tower*
La Tour Eiffel est une merveille architecturale.
The Eiffel Tower is an architectural marvel.

tourner   *to turn*
Pour venir chez moi, continuez tout droit et puis tournez à
    gauche.
To come to my house, go straight and then turn left.

tout(es, tous) m. (f., pl.)   *all, every*
Tous mes amis aiment bien le café mais moi je préfère le thé.
All my friends like coffee, but I prefer tea.

tous les deux   *both*
Je les aime tous les deux.
I like both of them.

traduction f.   *translation*
Quelle est la bonne traduction pour cette phrase?
What is the correct translation of this sentence?

traduire   *to translate*
Pouvez-vous traduire ces mots?
Can you translate these words?

tranche f.   *slice, piece*
Donne-leur deux tranches de pizza.
Give them two slices of pizza.

tranquille   *calm, quiet, peaceful*
Je cherche un endroit tranquille dans la bibliothèque pour
    étudier.
I'm looking for a quiet place in the library to study.

travail m.   *work, job*
Elle cherche un travail parce que son enterprise va bientôt fermer.
She's looking for another job because her business is going to close soon.

travailler *to work*
Les employées dans ce bureau détestent travailler le weekend.
The employees in this office hate working on weekends.

travers (à) *through, across*
Elle voyage à travers le monde pour prendre des photos pour son livre.
She's traveling around the world to take pictures for her book.

traverser *to cross*
Traverser l'Atlantique seul en bateau me semble très difficile.
Crossing the Atlantic alone in a boat seems very difficult to me.

très *very*
Après avoir fait du vélo dans cette chaleur il a très soif.
After biking in this heat he's very thirsty.

triste *sad*
Elle sera triste quand tu lui diras les nouvelles.
She'll be sad when you tell her the news.

trop *too much*
Elle a trop parlé.
She said too much.

trouver *to find*
Nous ne trouvons jamais son adresse avec notre GPS.
We never find his address with our GPS.

trouver, se *to be located*
Où se trouve ta maison?
Where is your house located?

truc m. *thing, thingamajig*
Il sert à quoi, ce truc?
What purpose does this thing serve?

tu *you (informal)*
Tu as quel âge, jeune homme?
How old are you, young man?

U

un(e) *one, a, an*
J'ai un frère / une sœur.
I have one brother / sister.

université (f.)   *university*
Meredith était professeur à l'Université de Paris X–Nanterre.
Meredith was a professor at the University of Paris X–Nanterre.

usine f.   *factory*
Les ouvriers en grève manifestent devant leur usine.
The striking workers are protesting in front of their factory.

utile   *useful*
Ce logiciel est très utile car il facilite certains calculs.
This software is very useful as it makes certain calculations easier.

utiliser   *to use*
Tu devrais utiliser cette crème hydratante pour ton visage.
You should use this moisturizer for your face.

V

vacances f. pl.   *vacation*
On a passé de très bonnes vacances en Tunisie l'année dernière.
We had a great vacation in Tunisia last year.

vagabonder   *to wander, to roam*
Il passe sa vie à vagabonder entre Londres et Paris.
He spends his life wandering between London and Paris.

vague f.   *wave*
Lorsque le vent souffle sur la surface du lac, cela crée des vagues.
When the wind blows on the surface of the lake, it creates a series of waves.

valise f.   *suitcase*
Cette vielle valise n'est plus fonctionnelle.
This old suitcase is no longer usable.

valoir   *to be worth*
Ça vaut combien?
How much is that worth?

vélo m.   *bike*
On va lui donner l'ancien vélo de notre fils.
We're going to give him our son's old bike.

vélo, faire du m.   *to go bike riding*
On fera du vélo s'il fait beau demain.
We'll go bike riding tomorrow if it's nice.

vendeur(-euse) m. (f.)   *shopkeeper, salesman, saleswoman*
Le vendeur nous a donné un rabais.
The salesman gave us a discount price.

vendre   *to sell*
Je veux vendre ma maison.
I want to sell my house.

venir   *to come*
Vous venez avec nous?
Are you coming with us?

vent m.   *wind*
Il y a du vent aujourd'hui.
It's windy today.

vérité f.   *truth*
Quelle est la vérité? On ne saura jamais.
What's the truth? We'll never know.

verre m.   *glass*
Vous voulez un verre de vin?
Do you want a glass of wine?
Cendrillon a porté une pantoufle de verre.
Cinderella wore a glass slipper.

vers   *toward, around*
Nous partons vers midi.
We're leaving around noon.

vert(e)   *green*
Tu devrais mettre une cravate verte avec ce costume noir.
You should wear a green tie with this black suit.

veste f.   *jacket*
Cette veste en cuir est vraiment démodée!
This leather jacket is really out of style!

vide   *empty*
Le bocal est vide, il n'y a plus de confiture.
The jar is empty; there's no more jam.

vie f.   *life*
La vie est belle.
Life is beautiful.

vieux(vieille) (viel in front of a vowel and *h)* old
Je regrette le bon vieux temps!
I miss the good old days!
Ce vieil immeuble est trop délabré.
This old building is too dilapidated.
Cette une vieille amie de ma mère.
She's an old friend of my mother's.

ville f. *city, town*
Quelle est la plus grande ville de cette région?
What is the biggest city in this region?

vitesse f. *speed*
Ce train roule à une très grande vitesse.
This train goes at a very high speed.

vivre *to live*
Elle rêve de vivre ailleurs, mais elle doit rester ici.
She dreams of living elsewhere, but she's stuck here.

voilà *here is, there is, here you go*
Et voilà une raison de plus pour ne plus lui faire confiance.
And here is one more reason to no longer trust her.

voir *to see*
Je veux voir le nouveau film de Scorsese, et toi?
I want to see Scorsese's new movie—how about you?

voisin(e) m. (f.) *neighbors*
Les nouveaux voisins semblent assez gentils.
The new neighbors seem nice enough.

voiture f. *car*
Quelle jolie voiture neuve, je suis jalouse.
What a beautiful new car—I'm jealous.

voix f. *voice*
Elle a perdu la voix à force de tousser toute la nuit.
She lost her voice from coughing all night.

vol m. *flight*
Leur vol part à minuit.
Their flight leaves at midnight.

voler *to fly; to steal*
Les frères Wright rêvaient de voler.
The Wright brothers dreamed about flying.
Les cambrioleurs ont volé mes bijoux.
The burglars stole my jewels.

voleur (-euse) m. (f.) *thief*
Voleur!
Thief!

vouloir *to want, to desire*
Après trois heures de route, elle ne va pas vouloir s'asseoir à
table pour trois heures de plus.
*After three hours on the road, she's not going to want to sit down at the
table for three more hours.*

vous *you, to you*
Vous êtes américain, non?
You're American, right?
Je vous appelle plus tard.
I'm going to call you later.

voyage m. *trip*
Elle n'est pas là; elle est en voyage.
She's not here; she's on a trip.

voyager *to travel*
Moi, j'aime bien voyager mais mon mari préfère rester à la
maison.
As for me, I like to travel, but my husband prefers to stay at home.

vraiment *really, truly*
Les joueurs sont vraiment fatigués après leur match de foot.
The players are really tired after their soccer game.

vue f. *sight, view*
Elle a une bonne vue alors que moi, je dois porter des lunettes.
She has good eyesight, whereas I need to wear glasses.

W

wagon-lit m. *sleeper car*
Il a horreur de dormir dans le wagon-lit, il préfère piquer un
roupillon dans son siège.
He hates sleeping in the sleeper car; he prefers to snooze in his seat.

Y

y   *there, it*

   Tu pars en Espagne? Oui, j'y vais tout de suite.
   Are you leaving for Spain? Yes, I'm going there right away.
   Je m'y attendais.
   I was expecting it.

yaourt m.   *yogurt*

   Elle refuse de manger le yaourt.
   She refuses to eat the yogurt.

yeux m. pl.   *eyes*

   J'ai mal aux yeux à cause de mes allergies.
   My eyes hurt because of my allergies.

Z

zouave m.   *clown, fool*

   Pourquoi tu fais toujours le zouave?
   Why do you always act like a clown?

Category Section

La Famille	The Family
beau-frère	brother-in-law
belle-sœur	sister-in-law
beau-père	father-in-law; stepfather
belle-mère	mother-in-law; stepmother
beau-fils	son-in-law; stepson
belle-fille	daughter-in-law; step-daughter
compagnon m.	partner, companion
copain	boyfriend
copine	girlfriend
conjoint(e)	spouse
cousin(e)	cousin
demi-frère	half-brother
demi-sœur	half-sister
femme	wife
fille	daughter
fils	son
frère	brother
grand-mère	grandmother
grand-père	grandfather
mari	husband
mère	mother
neveu	nephew
nièce	niece

oncle	uncle
partenaire m. / f.	partner
père	father
petits-enfants	grandchildren
petit-fils	grandson
petite-fille	granddaughter
sœur	sister
tante	aunt

Les Jours de la semaine — **Days of the Week**

lundi m.	Monday
mardi m.	Tuesday
mercredi m.	Wednesday
jeudi m.	Thursday
vendredi m.	Friday
samedi m.	Saturday
dimanche m.	Sunday

Les Mois — **Months of the Year**

janvier m.	January
février m.	February
mars m.	March
avril m.	April
mai m.	May
juin m.	June
juillet m.	July
août m.	August
septembre m.	September
octobre m.	October
novembre m.	November
décembre m.	December

Les Saisons — **The Seasons**

printemps m.	spring
été m.	summer

| automne m. | | fall |
| hiver m. | | winter |

Les Nombres	Numbers	Les Nombres	Numbers
zero	0	dix	10
un	1	onze	11
deux	2	douze	12
trois	3	treize	13
quatre	4	quatorze	14
cinq	5	quinze	15
six	6	seize	16
sept	7	dix-sept	17
huit	8	dix-huit	18
neuf	9	dix-neuf	19
vingt	20	soixante	60
vingt et un	21	soixante-dix/septante (Swiss)	70
vingt-deux	22	quatre-vingts/huitante (Swiss)	80
vingt-trois	23	quatre-vingts-dix/nonante (Swiss)	90
vingt-quatre	24	cent	100
vingt-cinq	25	cent un	101
vingt-six	26	deux cents	200
vingt-sept	27	trois cents	300
vingt-huit	28	cinq cents	500
vingt-neuf	29	mille	1 000
trente	30	deux mille	2 000
trente et un	31	vingt mille	20 000
quarante	40	cent mille	100 000
cinquante	50	un million	1 000 000

L'Heure

Il est dix heures.

Il est trois heures et demi.

Telling Time

It's ten a.m.

It's half past three.

Il est vingt-deux heures.	It's ten p.m.
Il est quatre heures moins le quart.	It's three forty-five.
Il est midi.	It's noon.
Il est deux heures et quart.	It's two-fifteen.
Il est minuit.	It's midnight.

Les Couleurs	Colors	Les Couleurs	Colors
la couleur	color	le noir	black
le blanc	white	l'orange	orange
le bleu	blue	le pourpre	purple
le brun	brown	le rose	pink
le gris	gray	le rouge	red
le jaune	yellow	le vert	green
le marron	chestnut	le violet	violet

Les Magasins	Shopping	Les Magasins	Shopping
bijouterie f.	jewelry store	magasin d'appareils-photo m.	camera store
blanchisserie f.	laundry	magasin de chaussures m.	shoe store
bureau de tabac m.	tobacco store	pâtisserie f.	pastry shop
boucherie f.	butcher's shop	pharmacie f.	pharmacy
boulangerie f.	bakery	poissonerie f.	fish shop
charcuterie f.	delicatessen	pressing m.	dry-cleaner
coiffeur, chez le m.	beauty salon, barber	quincaillerie f.	hardware store
grand magasin m.	department store	supermarché m.	supermarket
librairie f.	bookstore	traiteur, chez le m.	take-out place

Les Ordinateurs et l'Internet		Computers and the Internet	
clavier m.	keyboard	lecteur MP3 m.	MP3 player
clé USB f.	flash drive	mèl m.	email
courriel m.	email	mot de passe m.	password

disque dur externe m.	external hard drive	navigateur m.	browser
données f. pl.	data	ordinateur m.	computer
envoyer un texto m.	to send a text message	ordinateur portable m.	laptop
fichier m.	file	portable m.	cellphone
imprimante f.	printer	souris f.	mouse
l'Internet	the Internet	SMS m.	text message
jeux video m.	pl. video games	télécharger	to download